Value Education

Value Education

JAGDISH CHAND

Former Deputy Director of Education and
Executive Director of the Delhi Bureau of Textbooks,
Delhi Administration

ANSHAH Anshah Publishing House

(2017, 2011, 2009, First Published 2007)

Rs. 750; US$ 30

ISBN: 978-81-8364-013-8

2023 *Reprint Edition*

Value Education

Published by:
ANSHAH PUBLISHING HOUSE
LG 18-19, Pankaj Central Market,
Patparganj, Delhi 110092
011 22235152/ 6152, 9650028065
info@shiprapublication.com
www.shiprapublication.com

Preface

The theme of the book acquires a special significance in the present day context and has been made part of curriculum for students of education in number of universities. The three themes — Values, Environment and Human Rights, were published in a combined volume in 2005 by Shipra Publications, but keeping in view demand and requirements of the market and students, publishers approached us to bring out each theme separately also and the proposal gladly accepted. I hope users will take its advantage.

Author has made use of various reports, publications, document — primary and secondary sources to make this book students' friendly and express thanks to their authors and publishers. Utmost care has been taken while compiling this book, and regret if there is any omission. It is suggested that students/teachers must consult reference books or encyclopedias to study the subject in deep.

Jagdish Chand

Contents

1

Values: Concept, Nature and Classification of Values

MEANING OF THE CONCEPT 'VALUE'

Apart from the religion preachers and spiritualists, the economists, educators, humanists, philosophers, political leaders, psychologists, social reformers, sociologists and thinkers have reflected upon the meaning and dimensions of the concept 'Value.' Although their views differ widely but all of them stress the significance of values at personal, national and global level.

In view of the divergence of opinion on the concept, the noted philosopher A.C. Garnett in *Religion and Moral Life* (1955) observed that on account of the ambiguity of the term 'Value,' it should be avoided except where the contextual meaning is clear. In this context, A. Maslow in *The Further Research of Human Nature* (1982) said, "Values are defined in many ways and mean different things to different people. As a matter of fact, it is so confusing semantically that I am convinced we will soon give up this catch-all word in favour of more precise and more operational definition."

Having quoted the above-mentioned views, it is observed that values are so deeply embedded in human thoughts and actions that it is extremely important to understand the essence underlying values. In view of this, views of some thinkers are given here.

1. John Dewey (1948) views value as, "The value means primarily to prize, to esteem, to appraise and to estimate. It means the act of cherishing something, holding it dear and also the act of passing judgement upon the nature and amounts of values as compared with something else."

2. In the words of C.F. Kluckhon (1959), "Value is a conception, emplicit or implicit, distinctive of an individual or characteristics of a group of the desirables which influence the selection, from the

available means and ends of action."

3. The *Dictionary of Education* (1959) defines values "as the things in which people are interested—things they want to desire to be or become; feel as obligatory, worship, or enjoy."

4. T. Pattern Parsons (1960) holds, "Value is an element of shared symbolic system which serves a criterion or standard for selection among the alternatives of orientation which are intrinsically open in a situation."

5. Kane (1962) states "Values are the ideals, beliefs, or norms which a society or the large majority of a society's members hold."

6. According to Cuber (1962), "Values are the ideas and beliefs which people cherish. These ideas contain or express the judgement which people have, of the relative importance of things."

7. J.L. Spaulding (1963) perceives values in terms of the involvement among the components of limited closed system which are essential for the integration of the system as constituted at the given time.

8. Zaleznik and David (1964) observe "Values as the ideas in the mind of men comparable to norms in that they specify how people should behave. Values also attach degrees of goodness to activities and relationships."

9. I.J. Lehner and N.J. Kube maintain (1967) that "Values are the integral part of personal philosophy of life which we generally mean the system of values by which we live. The philosophy of life includes our aims, ideals and manner of thinking and the principles by which we guide our behaviour and conduct our affairs."

10. According to T.W. Hipple (1969), "Values are conscious or unconscious motivators and justifiers of the actions and judgement."

11. Rokeach (1973) defines values, "As an enduring belief, a specific mode of conduct or end along a continuum of relative importance."

12. M.P. Hunt (1975) looks at values "as a judgement concerning the worth of an object, person, group or situation. Value judgement contains evaluative rating terms, such as good, bad, moral, immoral, beautiful, ugly etc."

13. E.S. Brightman (1978) says, "In the most elementary sense, value means whatever is actually liked, prized, esteemed, desired, approved or enjoyed by any one at a time."

14. In *Teaching Values in College* (1980), R. Morrill has stated, "Although values cannot be defined through deeds, they always are mediated through specific acts."

N. Torralba (1995) has observed in *The Always of All Education: Values and Virtues*, "that values can be defined operationally to include norms of right conduc and good intellectual and moral habits."

15. P.N. Kirpal (1982) proposes for "a fresh enunciation of human values which can be shared by all and made operative in order to build human solidarity for greater justice and higher quality of life."

16. N.K. Dutt (1986) says that "a value is defined as an endeavour which satisfies need system, psychological as well as physiological needs. Almost all human beings have the same physiological needs but differ in their psychological needs, hence differ in their values and styles of life."

17. W.H. Kilpatrick has explained the concept of values as, "That out of man's capacity for goal seeking behaviour arise his wants and efforts and out of these come in consciously chosen ends (goals). Because ends conflict, man is led to weigh his goals against each other; when this is done critically enough values emerge."

18. Henderson in this context observes, "It has been pointed out that man acts to satisfy his wants, anything which satisfies a human want becomes thereby a value. To say that our conduct is motivated by our value is another way of saying that we act to satisfy our wants."

19. According to R.B. Perry, "That which is an object of interest is invested with value."

20. In the words of J.S. Brubacher, "To state one's aim of education is to state one's educational values."

21. R. Borsodi states, "Values are emotional judgements. They are generated by feelings not cognitions. They are emotional, not intellectual judgements."

22. D.W. Prall observes, "Value is precisely the term applied in common usage to objects which stand at the outer end of the relation called liking, the inner end of which is a human mind that likes."

23. According to Prof. C. Seshadri (1992), "Value refers to objects that human beings consider desirable and worthy of pursuit in their thoughts, feelings and actions. These objects may be material or abstract qualities and states of mind and heart like truthfulness, happiness, peace, justice. In any case, they function as ideals and standards and govern human actions."

24. Dr. (Ms.) R. Indira (1992) defines value as, "Value is a conception, explicit or implicit, and distinctive of an individual or of a group, of the desirable which influences the selection from the available modes, means and ends of an action. In other words, value

is an enduring belief that a specific mode of conduct or state of existence is personally or socially preferable to an opposite or converse mode of conduct or state of existence."

25. The Committee on Religious and Moral Instruction (1959) defined moral and spiritual values as: "Anything that helps us to behave properly towards others is moral value."

"Anything that takes us out of our self, and inspires us to sacrifice for the good of others or for a great cause is spiritual value."

26. Kireet Joshi (1997), a former Educational Adviser to the Government of India in *Education for Character Development* has explained the word "Value" in these words, "This word value as understood in the context of educational philosophy, refers to those desirable ideals and goals which are intrinsic in themselves and which, when achieved or attempted to be achieved, evoke a deep sense of fulfilment to one or many or all parts of what we consider to be the highest elements of our nature. In a sense, it may be urged that the word "value" is basically undefinable, since it denotes a fundamental category and it is itself the highest genius of that category." Truth, Beauty and Goodness are the supreme values of life. The author further observes, "At the same time, there is a common understanding in regard to truth, beauty and goodness which can be conceived as the supreme values of life. They are intrinsic in character and they are ends-in-themselves." It is contended by the same writer that "Even if there are wide differences as to what is meant by these three terms, there is agreement that they are most desirable ideals and mere orientation towards them inspires development of those states of our being and becoming in which we can hope to find some kind of ultimate fulfilment."

ORIGIN OF THE CONCEPT VALUES

A German philosopher Friedrich Nietzsche (1844–1900) is said to have used the word 'Values' first in 1880. Till then, the word 'Value' was used as a singular noun, meaning the measure of something, for example, the value of labour, money or labour. It was also used as a verb, meaning to value as esteem something. Nietzsche used the word 'Values' in plural to denote moral attitudes and beliefs that were personal and subjective. It is of interest to note that he along with several other thinkers believed that 'values' were not necessarily conducive for building strong personalities. In the modern democratic societies values are considered indispensable. Thus since then, the concept 'Values' has undergone radical change.

VALUES, VIRTUES, MORALITY AND ETHICS

Prof. B. Mukhopadhyay in his write-up in "*University News*" (March 7–13, 2005) has attempted to differentiate value related terms. He has observed, ".....Values do not mean only virtues. Moral values are known as virtues. Ethics deal with right and norms. Ethics is a system or code of morals. Once someone knows his values and knows what is important to him, ethics can help him to set goals."

Values involve individual feelings, ideas and beliefs an individual operates according to a system of values. Everything he does, every decision he makes, comes from within, conscious or unconscious system of values.

The Committee on Moral Education, Uttar Pradesh (1983), considers moral education and value-oriented education as one and the same thing. It, in its report on moral education, has given a wider meaning to it. It has interpreted it "to include not only ethical values but also spiritual, scientific, aesthetic and sporting values, indeed all humanistic values."

Education in Values: A Source Book, published by NCERT (1992) states, "The phrase 'value education' is preferred to other terms in vogue like 'moral education,' 'moral and spiritual education,' etc., in view of its comprehensiveness, the concern is with the development of values in general and that covers moral, social, spiritual, aesthetic and other values as well."

NATURE OF VALUES

1. Values are the standards or guidelines for an individual's life.
2. Values are influenced by an individual's experiences, desires and specific situations.
3. Values are the standards or guidelines for a nation that guide its policies.
4. Values steer our life's journey.
5. Values are not static.
6. Values are modes of organising conduct.
7. Values are acquired sub-consciously in many ways.

8. Values possess both cognitive and effective dimensions.
9. Values can be structured and restructured through processes of reflective thinking.
10. Values animate an individual. They move him around in his environment as they define its attractive and repelling sectors.
11. Values energise individuals to action.
12. Values are organised into value systems. The total number of values that constitute an individual's value system is not very large.
13. The value of a thing is on account of the fact that the thing has the power to satisfy our desires.
14. Anything has a value if it relates to the purpose of an individual which he has in his life.
15. Anything which has utility has value.
16. Values are felt sometimes partly and sometimes wholly.
17. Values are helpful for survival.
18. Anything which is helpful in organising society is called value.
19. Values are influenced by emotions.
20. Values are derived from several sources.

PHILOSOPHY OF VALUES

The philosophy of values is described by Swami Vivekananda in these words, "To be happy is the universal urge of all beings and at all times. One has to be at peace with oneself to be happy. These can be no peace for a turbulent mind. '*Vasanas*' (undesirable, wants) take away the peace of mind. It is only when we follow a value system that we can have a serene, contemplative mind. When mind is calm, we can turn it within to 'see' the treasure of pure consciousness. No treasure, on earth is equal to a slice of that '*tattva*' (element)."

'*Shrimad Bhagavat Gita*' states, "Mind, has to be loosened from '*durtyapara*' (misdeeds) and engaged in acquiring '*sadgunas*' (virtues). A mind which has '*daivi sampati*' (divine qualities) has '*Shanti*' (peace). These values make us introspective and correct our personality." About two thousand years ago, Thiruvalluvar a great saint said, "Achievement of a human being is proportionate to how high he or she thinks."

Einstein, one of the greatest scientists of the world has observed,

"A positive aspiration and effort for an ethical and moral configuration of our common life is of overriding importance. Here, no science can save us. I believe, indeed, solely the practical and factual in our education has led directly to the importance of ethical values."

In the words of our first Prime Minister, Pt. Jawaharlal Nehru, "Let us pursue our path to industrial progress with all our strength and vigour and at the same time remember that material riches without tolerance and compassion and wisdom may turn to dust and ashes."

CONFUSION OVER MEANING OF VALUES

- Values mean different things to different people.
- Value is what an individual desires likes or prefers.
- The range of values of man is indeed wide from mundane and petty desires to lofty ideals.
- Values depend upon the stage of development of a society.
- Values depend upon religious considerations.
- Values depend upon social systems.
- Values depend upon political systems.
- Values depend upon technologies.

CLASSIFICATION OF VALUES

Values are classified in a number of ways. However, here we are giving important types of classification.

Classification of Values I

1. Aesthetic values
2. Cultural values
3. Citizenship values
4. Economic or material values
5. Emotional values
6. Ethical values
7. Humanistic values
8. Intellectual or mental values
9. Moral values
10. National values
11. Physical values
12. Religious values

13. Scientific values
14. Social or sociological values
15. Spiritual values
16. Universal values
17. Positive values and negative values

It may be observed that there is no watertight compartmental classification of values as they overlap.

Classification or Types of Values II

- Intrinsic values
  - Values which are pursued for their own sake such as:
    1. Truth
    2. Goodness
    3. Beauty
- Instrumental or Mundane values
  - Cultural values (Conservation and promotion of culture)
  - Institutional values (Establishment, moral and political values)
  - Personal values (Values for the good of the individual)
  - Social values (Good of the society)

Classification III

- (1) National Values
- (2) Global Values

Classification IV

- (1) National Values
- (2) Individual Values

Classification V

- (1) Individual Values
- (2) Global Values

Classification VI

(1) Cultural Values

(2) Essential Values

(3) Personal Values

(4) Social Values

(5) Institutional Values

Classification VII

(1) Cultural Values

(2) Disciplinary Values

Classification VIII

(1) Liberalising Values

(2) Sentimental Values

Classification IX

(1) Preparatory Values

(2) Introductory Values

(3) Practical or utilitarian Values

(4) Conventional Values

Classification X

(1) Traditional Values

(2) Modern Values

Classification XI

(1) Material Values

(2) Non-material Values

Classification XII

(1) Religion Values

(2) Secular Values

Classification XIII

(1) Secular Values

(2) Scientific Values

Classification XIV

(1) Ethical Values

(2) Spiritual Values

Classification XV

(1) Positive Values

(2) Negative Values

Classification of Values XVI

Cognitive
Implying the knowledge that realisation of the 'true self' (Atman) is the real truth (*satya*)

Affective
Conveying that men have *Atma* (true self) leading to the concept of universal love (*Prem*) and inner peace or serenity (*shanti*) and equanimity under all situations

Conative
Doing one's duty calmly and sincerely without any thought of reward and personal gain which can be termed as righteous conduct (*Dharma*) in a non-violent manner.

Classification of Values: Core Values XVII

- Righteous conduct
- True love for others
- Non-violence
- Peace
- Truth

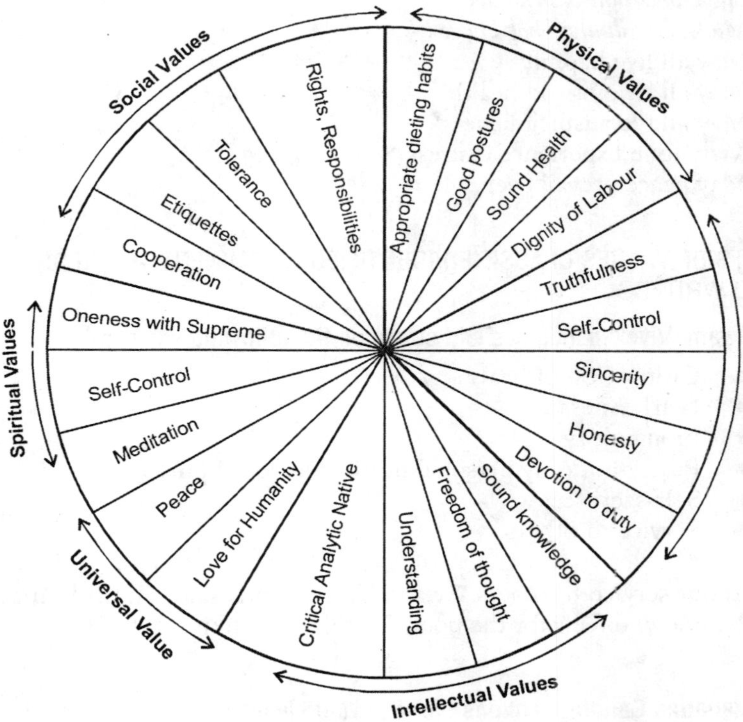

Fig. 1.1: Human Values

Modern vs. Traditional Values

- Modern democratic values and traditional colonial values
- Modern socialist values and traditional capitalist values
- Modern secular values and traditional religious values
- Modern scientific values and traditional spiritual values
- Modern global values and traditional national values
- Modern material values and traditional spiritual values.

Values as Enshrined in Indian Invocation

The following values enshrined in an ancient Indian Invocation are equally relevant even today.

Sarve bhavantu sukhinath
Sarve santu niramayah

Sarve bhadrani pashyantu
Ma kaschit dukha bhag bhavet!
May all live happily
May all enjoy good health
May all see auspiciousness
May none experience distress
May peace prevail everywhere!

LISTS OF VALUES CLASSIFIED/IDENTIFIED BY EMINENT THINKERS AND WRITERS

1. Swami Vivekananda has laid stress on the following values:

- Cultivation of heart
- Fearlessness
- Non-injury
- Purity not only personal purity, but social purity
- Self-sacrifice
- Service to others

About service to others, Swami Vivekananda said, "I call him a Mahatma who feels for the poor. Service to mankind is the highest goal."

2. Mahatma Gandhi mentions the following eleven values:

(1) '*Ahimsa*' (Non-violence)
(2) '*Satya*' (Truth)
(3) '*Astayam*' (Non-thriving)
(4) '*Brahmacharya*' (Purity)
(5) '*Aparigraha*' (Non-acquisitiveness)
(6) '*Sharirshrama*' (Physical work)
(7) '*Aswada*' (Control of Palate)
(8) '*Sarvatra Bhavjavarjana*' (Fearlessness)
(9) '*Sarva Dharma Sambhava*' (Looking up at all religious equally—toleration)
(10) '*Swadeshi*' (Patriotism—love of one's own country)
(11) '*Sparsha Bhavna*' (Abolition of untouchability).

3. Values emphasised at the National Seminar held at Coimbatore by Ramakrisha Mission Vidyalaya (Feb., 1980)

(1) Cleanliness

(2) Community service
(3) Compassion
(4) Dignity of labour
(5) Dutifulness
(6) Faith in God
(7) Integrity
(8) Fearfulness
(9) Non-violence
(10) Orderliness
(11) Patriotism
(12) Punctuality
(13) Respect for elders
(14) Respect for all religions
(15) Self-discipline
(16) Social responsibility
(17) Sound health
(18) Truthfulness (honesty).

4. Values suggested by Dr. Karan Singh, a great scholar and thinker, Chancellor, Jawaharlal Nehru University

In a write-up in the '*Hindustan Times*' December 10, 2004, Dr. Karan Singh referred to the following values:

(1) Family values
(2) Societal values
(3) Environmental values
(4) Inter-religious understanding values
(5) Spiritual values
(6) Global values.

The first relates to family values. By this I do not mean a reversion to conservative or retrogressive social structures. What I speak of is the necessity for harmony within the family, which, after all, is every child's first classroom. If there is conflict within the family, the effect on the child will be negative. Family values, such as respect for elders, helpfulness, cooperation and mutual affection, can go a long way in laying the foundations for a positive mindset. True, our educational system does not reach out to families, but that is where the first elements of education are inculcated, and where parent-teacher associations have an important role to play.

The second set of societal values include courtesy, consideration to strangers, punctuality, cleanliness and cooperation. After the family, it is the school or college where these values need to be inculcated. Involving students in the maintenance of the campus or in socially productive work is an excellent training for inter-cultural understanding. In developing nations like India, we have introduced the concept of socially productive work which involves students making periodic visits to slums or villages in the vicinity and assisting in projects designed to improve the standards of living.

The third set involves environmental issues. It is now well known that the 20th century witnessed a massive exploitation of the biosphere. If this trend continues, the prospect for the very survival of the human race may itself be brought into question. It is, therefore, necessary that the students develop an awareness of the importance of preserving and improving the environment.

The fourth set of values involves inter-religious understanding. Religion in history had had a mixed record. On the one hand, much that is great and noble in human civilisation — architecture, painting, literature, moral codes and social organisations — can be traced back to the great religions. On the other hand, more people have been persecuted in the name of religion than for any other reason. We can no longer afford to have endless conflicts in the name of religion. The key to inter-religious understanding lies in the acceptance of multiple paths to the divine. It is important that interfaith education should become part of curricula around the world.

This brings me to the fifth set of values — spiritual values. I am making a distinction between religion and spirituality, although they are closely intertwined. Spirituality attempts to access the divine power that resides within the deeper processes of our consciousness. It is this inner light that we all need to access, whether through prayer, meditation, *yoga*, *zen*, *tao*, *zikr* or any other methodology.

Finally, we need shared values for the emerging global society. As global citizens committed to human survival or welfare, we must use the latest array of innovative and interactive pedagogic methodologies to structure a worldwide programme of education.

5. Moral components advocated by John Wilson

(1) *A consideration for others*: — Principle of equality-dignity of the individual-virtues involved; kindness, sympathy, altruism, courtesy, cooperation etc.

(2) *An awareness of feelings in one's own and in others*: — capacity to anticipate the feelings that would arise in himself and in others as a result of his action-moral thinking about the pros and cons of his action—"Do unto others as you would like them do unto you"—virtues involved: magnanimity, nobility, altruism etc.

(3) *Ability to collect data* (in a situation involving morality)—right decision making—moral issues and moral conflicts—ability to collect all relevant facts—analyse—think of the possible course of action—scientific method of solving problems—virtues involved: reasoning, endurance, patience, etc.

(4) *Ability to take a decision*:— moral education must train the person to be able to take the right decision – virtues involved: justice, wisdom, temperance etc.

(5) *Will to act on the decision*:— may not act for want of sufficient courage—fear anticipated—virtues involved: courage, duty, responsibility etc.

6. List of the Values as Compiled by NCERT

The list compiled by the NCERT on the basis of various documents on education as well as the study of the Gandhian literature as given in Appendix III of "*Documents on Social, Moral and Spiritual Values in Education*" (1979) is given below:

(1) Abstinence
(2) Appreciation of cultural values of others
(3) Anti-untouchability
(4) Citizenship
(5) Consideration for others
(6) Concern for others
(7) Cooperation
(8) Cleanliness
(9) Compassion
(10) Common cause
(11) Common Good
(12) Courage
(13) Courtesy
(14) Curiosity
(15) Democratic Decision Making
(16) Devotion
(17) Dignity of the Individual
(18) Dignity of Manual Work
(19) Duty
(20) Discipline
(21) Endurance
(22) Equality
(23) Friendship
(24) Faithfulness
(25) Fellow-feeling
(26) Freedom

(27) Forward Look
(28) Good Manners
(29) Gentlemanliness
(30) Gratitude
(31) Honesty
(32) Helpfulness
(33) Humanism
(34) Hygienic living
(35) Initiative
(36) Integrity
(37) Justice
(38) Kindness
(39) Kindness to animals
(40) Loyalty to duty
(41) Leadership
(42) National consciousness
(43) National integration
(44) National unity
(45) Non-violence
(46) Obedience
(47) Patriotism
(48) Peace
(49) Proper utilisation of time
(50) Punctuality
(51) Purity
(52) Quest for knowledge
(53) Regularity
(54) Resourcefulness
(55) Respect for Others
(56) Reverence for old age
(57) Secularism and respect for all religions
(58) Self-confidence
(59) Self-control
(60) Self-discipline
(61) Self-duty
(62) Self-help
(63) Self-reliance
(64) Self-respect
(65) Self-restraint
(66) Self-support
(67) Sense of discrimination
(68) Sense of social responsibility between good and bad
(69) Simple living
(70) Sincerity
(71) Socialism
(72) Social justice
(73) Social service
(74) Solidarity of mankind
(75) Spirit of enquiry
(76) Sympathy
(77) Team spirit
(78) Team work
(79) Tolerance
(80) Truthfulness
(81) Universal love
(82) Universal truth
(83) Value for national and civic property.

7. **S.J. Dackawish in *Analysis of Values of Modern Age Midwerborn Community. Sociology and Social Research* (1959) lists the following 12 basic values:**

(1) Fairness
(2) Genuineness
(3) Happiness
(4) Humility
(5) Impulsive control
(6) Integrity
(7) International skills
(8) Love for people

(9) Mentality (10) Religion
(11) Respect for dignity (12) Sobriety.

8. The White House Conference on Education (1955) laid stress on the following values:

- Appreciation of our democratic heritage
- Ability to think and evaluate consistently and creatively.
- Ethical behaviour based on a sense of moral and spiritual values.
- Wise use of time, including constructive leisure pursuits.
- An awareness of our relationships with the world community.

9. Berelson and Salter. (1972) divide values in the following two categories:

- *Values of Heart*. These include—adventure, affection, idealism, independence, justice and patriotism.
- *Values of Mind*. These consist of—domination, economic success, personal success, power, problem solving competence and social security.

10. Thomas's (1967) classifies Values into six groups:

(1) Aesthetic values
(2) Humanitarian values
(3) Intellectual values
(4) Power values
(5) Material values, and
(6) Religious Values.

11. Weil and Weid (1971) divide values into three main categories:

(1) *People oriented values* like case, concern, cooperation and helpfulness.
(2) *Extension values* like money, security, status, etc.
(3) *Expressive values* like opportunities using special abilities and aptitudes.

12. Some Scholars Like Roheach (1973) classify values in two broad categories:

(1) Instrumental values (2) Terminal values.

A person having instrumental may be:

(1) Ambitious (2) Broadminded
(3) Capable (4) Cheerful

(5) Clean
(6) Courageous
(7) Forgiving
(8) Helpful
(9) Honest
(10) Imaginative
(11) Independent
(12) Intellectual
(13) Logical
(14) Loving
(15) Obedient
(16) Polite
(17) Responsible
(18) Self-controlled.

The terminal values of a person consist of the following characteristics:

(1) Beauty
(2) Comfortable life
(3) Equality
(4) Exciting life
(5) Equality
(6) Family security
(7) Freedom
(8) Happiness
(9) Inner security
(10) National security
(11) Self-respect
(12) Sense of accomplishment
(13) Social recognition
(14) True friendship
(15) Wisdom.

13. Hunt (1975) lists the following values in the modern age:

(1) Concern for egualitarianism
(2) Concern for free speech
(3) Concern for peaceful resolution of disputes
(4) Concern for participatory democracy
(5) Concern for freedom in personal life style
(6) Disdain for traditional political interests
(7) Concern for natural environment
(8) Concern for natural human values.

Hunt further suggests that the recommendations of the White House Conference on Education (1955) hold valid even today.

14. Jangira (1985) classifies values into the two groups as under:

1. *Core values* consisting of mutual trust, faith in the goodness of man, social courtesises leading to mutual respect, pursuit of excellence in work, appreciation of aesthetics, supporting the just cause, truthfulness, etc.
2. *Ethical values* comprising hard work, regularity, punctuality, respect for teachers, concern for the prestige of the institution, avoidance of telling lies for the petty gains, smoking, drinking, gambling, stealing and copying.

15. V.S. Mathur lists the following values of Indian Culture:

1. Avoiding extremes
2. Receptivity to learn
3. Spiritual approach to life
4. Taking comprehensive view of life
5. Tolerance.

16. V.K. Gokak (1982) has classified the values as:

1. Truth
2. Righteous conduct
3. Peace
4. Love
5. Non-violence.

17. The Parliamentary Standing Committee on Human Resource Development on Values

Eighty First Report on Value Based Education (1999) (Chavan Committee's Report) submitted in both Houses of Parliament observed that *Truth (Satya), Righteous conduct (Dharma), Peace (Shanti), Love (Prema) and Non-violence (Ahimsa) are the Core Universal Values which can be identified as the foundation stone on which the value based education programmes can be built up.*

18. 'National Curriculum Framework for School Education' (2000)

It has observed, "Truth, righteous conduct, peace, love and non-violence are the core universal values that can become the foundation for building the value based education programme.... These five universal values represent the five domains of human personality–intellectual, physical, emotional, psychological and spiritual—are correlated with the five major objectives of education, namely knowledge, skill, balance, vision and identity." In addition, key qualities like regularity, punctuality, cleanliness, self-control, industriousness, sense of duty, desire to serve, responsibility, enterprise, sensitivity to equality, fraternity, democratic attitude and sense of obligation to environmental protection have been highlighted. The Frame Work has proposed inculcation and nurturance of moral, ethical, humanistic and constitutional values.

VALUE OF VALUES

Instrumental Values. A subject is said to have instrumental value when it is pursued, not for its own sake, but for some ends beyond itself. Instrumental values include preparatory or introductory, practical or utilitarian, socialising and conventional values.

A subject is said to have a *Preparatory* value when it prepares the way for other studies. Arithmetic prepares the way for Algebra. When a particular study introduces us to a number of subjects, it has an *introductory* value. It is identical with the preparatory value. To illustrate we may select Physical Geography which introduces us to a little of Botany, Zoology, Physics and Chemistry. The *practical or utilitarian* value lies in a study of subject whose pursuit is useful inasmuch as it satisfies many wants and needs. The subject is individually and directly practical when the knowledge of the subject is applied directly by the person himself. A person may use his knowledge of hygiene to escape small pox. The same knowledge can, however, be used through other agencies, through society, for example. A subject is said to possess a socialising value when it creates socially desirable habits and reactions, or when it enables us to understand society in its complexities. The *socialising value* includes moral values too. These moral values refer to certain moral traits that society wants individuals to develop. The *conventional value* implies a value which is conventionally desirable in a subject. Certain subjects may be studied because their knowledge is expected of people of a certain class. Their knowledge is indeed for proper social intercourse and social enjoyment. In the times of Locke, a gentleman was expected to learn Latin, Greek and Grammar because they were necessary in that social set up.

Intrinsic values are inherent in the subjects that we may describe as cultural studies. These have been described by Dewey as the appreciative studies. The resulting experiences in these subjects are worthwhile on their own account. These values that accrue from their studies are in the form of aesthetic pleasures or intellectual joys. According to Wright, "An intrinsic value is of worth on its own account; an instrumental value because of its consequences." Examples of intrinsic values are truth, beauty and goodness, etc. They themselves are the ends and not the means for achieving some other end.

The *cultural values* have been subdivided into the *liberalising* and the *sentimental values*. The liberalising value consists in the pleasure that accompanies intellectual insight. The sentimental value, on the other hand, refers to pleasure that emerges when our feelings are exercised. Our feelings may be aroused by the aesthetic, the comic, the social and the moral situation. Drama, Literature, Music, Painting, Sculpture and Religion have, in varying degrees, these values.

Professor Cunningham lays stress on the disciplinary values of the subjects. Their pursuit is important because it gives rise to mental activity and forms sound habits and skills. Each subject, he says, causes certain type of mental operation or discipline. For example, natural sciences produce an attitude of mind characterised by precision which results from observation and reflective thinking. The humanistic sciences produce the discipline of tolerance. Metaphysical sciences, theology and philosophy produce the discipline of unification because in all these the ultimate aim is to achieve harmony and unity in life. The discipline of appreciation is produced by such subjects as painting, music, sculpture and others. The language will produce the discipline of expression which consists not only in the training to express oneself but also in being able to understand what others say and write.

Essential Values. These values involve the basic nature of man himself and include elementary physical skills, basic social skills, ability to use symbols such as language and numbers.

Personal Values. These values make a person good for himself.

Social Values. These values are good for the society and form the basis of the relationship of an individual with other people in society.

Institutional Values. These include values established by institutions-political etc.

Global Values. These values pertain to the entire humanity.

Ethical Values. These relate to our personal behaviour with our fellow-beings. Among these we include values like honesty and truth etc. All moral values are also covered under ethical values.

National Values. These include values relating to national goals, i.e., democratic, secular and socialist.

Spiritual Values. These are concerned with the realisation of the 'Self' and being one with 'Divinity.'

Note: All values overlap to some degree. No rigid classification is possible.

SYNTHESIS BETWEEN THE TRADITIONAL VALUES AND MODERN VALUES

In the attempt to inculcate values through education, we should draw freely upon our own traditions as well as the traditions of other countries and cultures of the world. There are strands within Indian thought itself which can lead to the new outlook appropriate for a modern society, and which can prepare the people for a willing acceptance of life with all its joys and sorrows, its challenges and triumphs. In them, too, we can find inspiration for social service and faith in the future. Mahatma Gandhi, for instance—and some other great leaders of thought—discovered the inspiration for their idealism and their passionate striving for social justice and social reconstruction largely from these sources. It is such re-interpretations and re-evaluations of the past that are now most needed. It is, however, specially important in the world of today that this effort should not be restricted to the national sources only. It would be necessary to draw upon liberalising forces that have arisen in the western nations and which have emphasised among other things, the dignity of the individual, equality and social justice.

India is on the move again with the promise of new renaissance in the making. The most powerful tool in the process of this renaissance and modernisation is education based on secular values on the one hand and on the other on science and technology. In this context we cannot do better than to quote Pt. Jawaharlal Nehru, "Can we combine the progress of science and technology with the progress of mind and spirit also? We cannot be untrue to science because that represents the basic fact of life today. Still less can we be untrue to those essential principles for which India has stood in the past throughout the ages. Let us then pursue our path to industrial progress with our strength and vigour and at the same time remember that material riches without toleration and compassion and wisdom may well turn to dust and ashes."

The Education Commission 1964–66 has observed, "We believe that India should strive to bring science and the values of the spirit together in harmony and thereby pave their way for the eventual emergence of a society which would cater to the needs of the whole man and not only to a particular fragment of his personality."

Remarks made by Albert Einstein in '*Ideas and Opinions*' in this regard are very enlightening: "It is not enough to teach man a speciality. Through it he may become a useful machine but not a harmoniously developed personality. It is essential that the students require an understanding of and a lively feeling for values. He must require a vivid sense of the beautiful and of the morally good. Otherwise he with his specialised knowledge resembles a well-trained dog rather than a harmoniously developed person."

CHARACTERISTICS OF PERSONS WITH MATERIAL VALUES AND SPIRITUAL VALUES

The materialistic persons hanker after money, power and prestige and for the achievement of this objective, they are prepared to go to any lengths. Plagued with suspicion of one another, they tend to become incapable of meaningful communication and deep personal relationships. They are prone to destructive and violent acts. They are very selfish. On the other hand, the spiritualists act on the premise that an individual is made for mutually helpful and satisfying relationships. They are pre-occupied with enlightenment and truth. Humility is the hallmark of their behaviour. Arrogance and pride are anathema to them. Their relationships are marked by honesty, integrity and openness.

2

Meaning and Need for Education of Human Values: Objectives of Education for Human Values

MEANING OF EDUCATION FOR HUMAN VALUES

Education for human values refers to the educational programme which is geared to the realisation of the vision of the society as envisaged in its Constitution for the good of the society and good life of the individual. It covers all aspects of the personality development — aesthetic, intellectual, moral, social and spiritual.

CHIEF CHARACTERISTICS OF EDUCATION FOR HUMAN VALUES

Following are the chief characteristics of the education for human values:

1. Value education is a comprehensive process.
2. Value education is a process of direct as well as indirect inculcation of proper habits, the development of proper attitudes, sensibilities and characters of the learners.
3. Value education is related to the good of 'every' learner and of 'whole' learner to serve as a powerful instrument of social and national reconstruction.
4. The process of value development is influenced by a host of environmental factors—home or the family, school, the peer group, community, the media and the general ethos of the society.

ROLE OF THE SCHOOL IN THE DEVELOPMENT OF THE HUMAN VALUES

Discussed separately

NEED FOR THE EDUCATION OF HUMAN VALUES

Values form an important element of the personality of individuals which influences their thought and behaviour in an unconscious manner. They are normative standards by which human beings are influenced in the choice among alternative courses of action. It is, therefore, very essential that education should develop such values in the students that they become an asset and guide them to become individuals of sterling character who place service of the society above service of the self.

C. Rajagopalachari (1879–1972) the first and the last Indian to occupy the position of Governor General of India and one of the most prominent statesmen of India has said, "National character is the keystone on whom rests the fate and future of our public affairs, not this 'ism'. National character depends on, and, in fact, is individual rectitude.

Individual honesty must be brought into being before we can hope for improvement of national affairs.

If the parched field of Indian politics and administration has to get fresh, green life and grow, we need the monsoon of purity in national character.

And the monsoon consists of little drops falling and uniting to make rain.

Individual purity of character alone can revive the parched field, let's regain our character quickly and all will be well — politics, administration and economic conditions." This exhortation assumes special significance now when the pace of progress of values has lagged behind the pace of progress of materialism.

The Committee on Religious an Moral Instruction (1959) explained the need for teaching moral and spiritual values as: We have to lay special stress on teaching of moral and spiritual values. Moral values particularly refer to the conduct of man towards man in the various situations in which human beings come together in the home, in social and economic fields, and in the life of the outside world generally. It is essential that from the earliest childhood, moral values should be inculcated in us. We have to influence the home first. We fear that our homes are not what they ought to be. Habits, both of mind and body, formed in the early years at home, persist and influence our life afterwards. Good manners are a very important part of moral education. It is not unusual that when a people attain freedom suddenly, after long years of bondage, they are inclined to become self-willed, arrogant and inconsiderate. In such situations good manners are easily set aside and young people tend to express the first flush of freedom in licence and rowdyism.

The importance of good manners cannot be overstressed. Good manners will impose proper restraint on us and remove harshness in our words and rudeness in our behaviour. Good manners verily are like the oil that helps keep the machine of human society running smoothly. We have been losing our manners rather rapidly and it is necessary that we should recover them. Good manners should be sedulously inculcated and teachers must give instruction in this to all students at all times, both by examples and by precept. We must be constantly told that what hurts us, hurts others also and we must behave towards others as we want others to behave towards us.

Then there is a great deal of talk of corruption and dishonesty in our official and business life. It is the students of today who are to be in charge of the various departments of life tomorrow; and if they learn what real integrity is in their early years, they are not likely to go very far wrong later on. Every effort must, therefore, be made to teach students true moral values from the earliest stage of their educational life. We are not unaware of the various steps that are being taken at different educational levels towards literacy drive, adult education, and education of the handicapped. If the content of education is also enriched with moral and spiritual values, the purpose of education will have been truly fulfilled.

Just as moral values affect the relations between man and man, so do spiritual values affect the individual in his relation with himself. The individual is not only a body; he is also a soul. He does not live by bread alone; he wants inner peace and happiness. If he loses all spiritual values, he loses the possibility of being at peace with himself. It is necessary to have some faith in things beyond the flesh, some identification with a purpose greater than oneself in order to achieve this mental equilibrium."

Martin Luther King said, "We have guided missiles and misguided men. This must be changed for the better by infusion of morality in private and public life."

Addressing the inspiring gathering of the religious and spiritual leaders, ever held at the UN in August-September 2000, the UN Secretary General called upon them to 'look within' and to consider what they could do to promote "justice, equality, reconciliation and peace."

There is no doubt that some sort of 'spiritual therapy' is needed for having a value based society and this need can be fulfilled to a considerable extent through education.

Value education in schools is needed for the development of balanced personalities who are:

1. Appreciative of good in others
2. Creative
3. Emotionally stable
4. Fair
5. Fearless
6. Happy and cheerful
7. Loyal (steadfast)
8. Patriotic
9. Productive
10. Self-confident
11. Self-controlled (disciplined)
12. Self-reliant
13. Silent (whenever needed)
14. Socially adjusted
15. Socially responsible

VALUES NEEDED TO BE INCULCATED AMONG SCHOOL STUDENTS

A. J.C. Verma has suggested the following values in "*Education for Self-Development*" (1983)

1. Care for public property
2. Cleanliness
3. Cooperativeness
4. Consideration of others
5. Freedom
6. Hard work
7. Honesty
8. Love for one's country
9. Justice
10. Non-violence
11. Scientific temper
12. Secularism

13. Self-discipline
14. Service to people
15. Team spirit
16. Truth.

B. M.T. Ramji in his book "*Value-oriented School Education,*" has suggested that the students should be encouraged to acquire the following values:

1. Cleanliness
2. Courage
3. Courtesy
4. Dignity of manual work
5. Joy
6. Manual work
7. Peace
8. Purity
9. Service
10. Truth
11. Universal love.

C. *C.B.S.E. and Value-oriented School Climate*

A Conference on Value Education (1986) organised by the Central Board of Secondary Education, Delhi identified the following 50 values which should form the school climate:

1. Respect for individual
2. Education for service rather than competition
3. Openness, freedom, flexibility
4. Human relationship
5. Participation with maximum involvement
6. Sensitivity and awareness
7. Concern for each other
8. Scientific attitude and scientific temper
9. Honesty and integrity
10. Value of time
11. Mature self
12. Self-acceptance, self-awareness, self-confidence
13. Understanding leading to forgiveness
14. Relationship with God

15. Individual yet socially responsible
16. Work ethics
17. Dignity of labour
18. Trust
19. Fearlessness
20. Moral courage
21. Tolerance/acceptance of difference
22. Practice before preaching
23. Compassion
24. Use of head, heart and hand
25. Acculturation
26. Patriotism
27. Communication
28. Environment preservation
29. Justice
30. Exposure to world and international understanding
31. Integrated development
32. Staff development
33. Pastoral care
34. Team spirit
35. Parent-teacher relationship
36. Developed potentials
37. Optimism, faith and hope
38. Vision and sense of purpose
39. Life-long learner
40. Innovativeness and resourcefulness
41. Creativity and initiative
42. Sense of belonging
43. Sense of pride
44. Risk taking
45. Sense of adventure
46. Dedication and commitment
47. Simplicity and austerity
48. Ability to set standards and stick to those
49. Adaptability
50. Attention to details.

OBJECTIVES OF EDUCATION FOR VALUES: UNESCO PROJECT

UNESCO-NIER Joint Report on *Moral Education in Asian*

Countries (1980) lists the following objectives of value (moral) education:

1. Full development of child's personality in its physical, mental, emotional and spiritual aspect.
2. Inculcation of good manners and of responsible and cooperative citizenship.
3. Developing respect for the dignity of the individual and sanctity of fundamental human rights.
4. Inculcation of a spirit of patriotism and national integration.
5. Developing a democratic way of thinking and living.
6. Developing tolerance towards and understanding of different religious faiths.
7. Developing a sense of human brotherhood at the social, national and international level.
8. Helping children to have faith in some supernatural power and order that is supposed to control this universe and human life (This belong to the communities of believers).
9. Enabling children to make moral decision on the basis of sound moral principles.

OBJECTIVES OF ETHICAL AND SOCIAL VALUES AS SUGGESTED BY THE NATIONAL SEMINAR HELD AT COIMBATORE BY RAMAKRISHNA MISSION VIDYALAYA (FEB. 1980)

The outcome of inculcating ethical and social values in education is envisaged to be the emergence of balanced personalities who are:

(i) Self-confident
(ii) Self-reliant
(iii) Self-controlled (disciplined)
(iv) Happy and cheerful
(v) Emotionally stable
(vi) Productive
(vii) Appreciative of good in others
(viii) Creative
(ix) Silent (whenever needed)
(x) Socially responsible
(xi) Socially adjusted
(xii) Fearless

(xiii) Fair
(xiv) Loyal (steadfast)
(xv) Patriotic

OBJECTIVES OF VALUE-ORIENTED EDUCATION IN SRI SATHYA SAI INSTITUTE OF HIGHER LEARNING, PRASANTHINILAYAM, ANDHRA PRADESH

1. To help the students cultivate self-knowledge and self-confidence, so that each one can learn self-sacrifice and self-realisation.
2. To make spiritual uplift, self-discovery, and social service the end of education through love and detachment.
3. To emphasise on giving and forgiving and not on getting and forgetting.
4. To encourage service, especially among the illiterate and the needy in the villages around.
5. To highlight the responsibilities of youth, rather than rights: for, the right is earned only by the proper discharge of the responsibility.
6. To inculcate detachment, loving service, fraternity, humility, sincerity, fortitude, self-reliance, independence and fearlessness.
7. To inculcate in the students respect for their culture and gratitude to their parents, villages, nation and all those who strive for their welfare.
8. To develop in the students: Love All—Serve All and Hurt Never—Help Ever mentality.
9. To make the students internalise the mental outlook, that education is for life and not for living wherein the end of education is character.
10. To shape the students into responsible citizens and impel/ motivate them to subordinate their individual interests before the national interests.

3

Five Universal Values and Their Sub-values as Listed by Gokak Committee

GOKAK'S CLASSIFICATION OF VALUES AND SUB-VALUES

V.K. Gokak classified and grouped values under the five basic human values.

Table 3.1: Five Basic Human Values and Their Sub-values

Truth	*Righteous Conduct*	*Peace*	*Love*	*Non-violence*
1. Curiosity	1. Cleanliness	1. Awareness of dignity of individual	1. Devotion	1. Appreciation of other's culture
2. Discrimination	2. Courage	2. Concentration	2. Friendship	2. Awareness of responsibility of citizenship
3. Quest for knowledge	3. Dignity of labour	3. Discipline	3. Humanism	3. Away from untouchability and national property
4. Reason	4. Duty and loyalty to duty	4. Endurance	4. Kindness to animals	4. Common good
5. Respect for all religions	5. Equality	5. Integrity	5. Patriotism	5. Compassion universal love
6. Secularism	6. Faithfulness	6. Meditation	6. Sincerity	6. Consideration for others
7. Spirit of enquiry	7. Hygienic living	7. Purity	7. Sympathy	7. Courtesy
8. Study of oneself	8. Honesty	8. Self-discipline	8. Tolerance	8. Fellow-feeling
9. Universal, self-existent truth	9. Justice	9. Self-respect		9. Gentlemanliness not to hurt
10. Truthfulness	10. Initiative			10. Good manners
	11. Proper utilisation of time			11. Helpfulness

(*Contd.*)

(Contd.)

Truth	Righteous Conduct	Peace	Love	Non-violence
	12. Prudence			12. Kindness
	13. Punctuality			13. National awareness
	14. Regularity			14. National integrity
	15. Resourcefulness			15. National unity
	16. Respect for others			16. Readiness to cooperate
	17. Reverence			17. Socialism
	18. Self-help			18. Social justice
	19. Self-confidence			19. Social service
	20. Self-reliance			20. Solidarity
	21. Self-sacrifice			
	22. Self-support			
	23. Service to others			
	24. Simple living			
	25. Team spirit			
	26. Teamwork			

Source: Gokak, V.K., *Teacher's Handbook for the Course in the Human Values* (1982).

ENUNCIATION OF FIVE VALUES

Sri Sathya Sai Institute of Higher Learning, Prasanthinilayam, Andhra Pradesh, has done a pioneering work in the field of human value education. Here, a brief description of Five Human Values as enunciated by the Institute is given.

The Sathya Sai Education in Human Values Programme (SSEHV) identifies 'Five Domains' of human personality and 'Five Basic Human Values' corresponding to these domains.

The five domains of the personality are the physical, intellectual, emotional, super-conscious and the spiritual.

The five "basic human values" are of Truth, Right Conduct, Peace, Love and Non-violence. They are called basic because they are pursued by people of all cultures and religions and they are timeless. They include the profound moral insights of the great civilisations; and they are derived from the universal order which upholds harmony in society. The values are called human because their practice makes one "human" in the true sense of the word.

These five basic values correspond with the five domains of the personality. The intellectual level corresponds with Truth; the physical level corresponds with Right Conduct; the emotional level corresponds with Peace; the Super-Conscious level corresponds with Love; and the Spiritual domain corresponds with Non-violence.

The five values are in turn the end result produced by the five domains of the human personality.

The intellect pursues and perceives the Truth.

The refinement of the human results in Righteous Conduct.

The elimination of the lower impulses results in Peace.

Love, which is defined as pure and selfless, flows forth from the Psyche itself and functions like intuition.

Non-violence, or universal love, is love which flows from a higher consciousness and identifies itself with each individual and object in the universe.

Thus the holistic development of the personality becomes possible when all these faculties of the human being are refined to perfection.

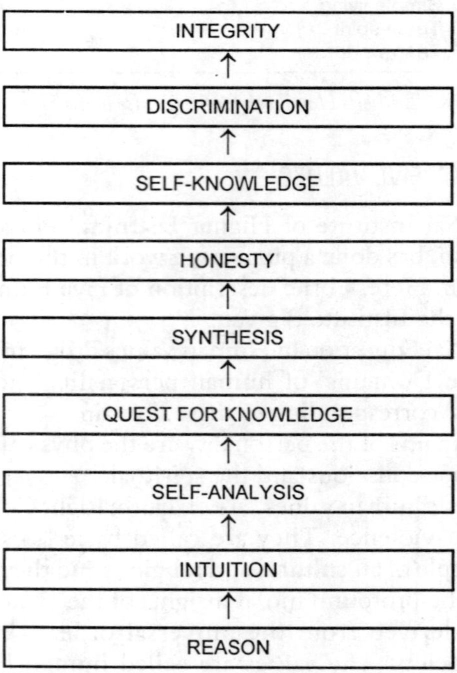

Fig. 3.1: Levels of Truth

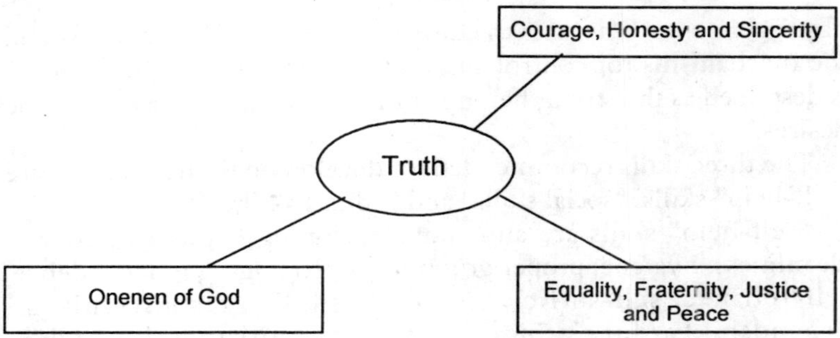

Fig. 3.2: Truth

Truth

Truth is considered the most important of the five human values. This is because if one recognises the Truth that all humanity is one with a Supreme Being, the practice of the four other values becomes automatic.

In the Human Values Programme, Truth is defined as the unison of thought, word and deed. It is also that which never changes and hence it is beyond causation. Furthermore, it is the awareness of the truth of Being. Lastly, truth is incapable of being destroyed. Since it corresponds with the intellectual domain, Truth represents the zenith of intellectual perfection and the blossoming of intuition in the individual. It is a testimony to the capacity of the intellect and the power and efficacy of intuition.

Components of Sub-values of Truth

In this Programme, Truth is developed through exposing children to components of Truth. These components are called 'sub-values' and they are curiosity, discrimination, equality, honesty, integrity, intuition, optimism, quest for knowledge, reason, self-analysis and truthfulness. These sub-values of Truth concretise the value for children and provide a focus for the teacher.

Right Conduct

Right Conduct is concerned with developing the physical level of personality, primarily because man uses his body to engage in action.

Within the context of the SSEHV programme, the physical does not only mean the development of a strong, healthy body. The physical also encompasses the development of skills and habits and the mechanisms for control and discipline. In fact, Right Conduct is described as the strengthening of the will so that it may direct the desires.

The three skills recommended for developing Right Conduct are "self-help" skills, "social skills" and "ethical skills."

"Self-help" skills are aimed at developing habits of personal cleanliness, hygiene, proper grooming, encouraging independence, self-reliance, self-sufficiency, responsibility, resourcefulness, dependability, duty, ethics, helpfulness, initiative, leadership, perseverance, proper use of time, self-confidence and simplicity.

"Social skills" enable the child to function successfully in the various groups in which he belongs. The child is therefore taught how to sit properly, to answer with respect, to work harmoniously with others, to obey the rules of a game, to listen to and respect the views and opinions of others and to await his turn, among other things. He must share with others and he must respect parents, teachers, elders and other persons in authority.

Closely related to 'social skills' is a third category—'ethical skills.' These skills are important both for personal character development and for interacting with others. Some of the skills emphasised are speaking pleasantly with others, speaking the truth, respect for the property of others and refraining from hurting others in thought, word and deed.

Right Conduct is based on the premise that each individual is regarded as a link in the chain of creation, and just as each link needs to be in good condition for the effective functioning of the chain, in the same way, each person's conduct should be perfect for the orderly functioning of the universe.

Peace

The practice of Right Conduct leads to Peace.

Peace is often described as the most elusive of the five values.

The reason for its elusiveness is that it is always sought in the external phenomena.

'Peace' as a value in the SSEHV Programme is conceptualised as being innate in man; it is within each person simply waiting to be uncovered.

It is described as 'inner mental calm,' 'mental equipoise' or 'equal-mindedness.'

Equanimity of mind is achieved when a person is able to switch from outward vision to inward vision and is consequently able to minimise his desires and achieve a greater degree of contentment.

'Peace' as described in the Programme does not mean being idle or inactive or absence of reaction. It is the calm contentment arising from the right attitude towards action. It is not static, it expresses itself in creative activities such as art, drama, dance, music and writing. These activities enable the child to express his energy in constructive ways.

Hence Peace is seen as a condition in which the child's energy works in coordination towards some worth-while or noble goal.

So that Peace might blossom within the child, the SSEHV programme aims at fostering the qualities of: attention, calmness, concentration, dignity, discipline, endurance, focus, happiness, honesty, humility, inner silence, optimism, patience, reflection, satisfaction, self-acceptance, self-confidence, self-control, self-discipline, self-respect and understanding. The development of these qualities results in the elimination of negative qualities and tendencies which cover the peace that lies within.

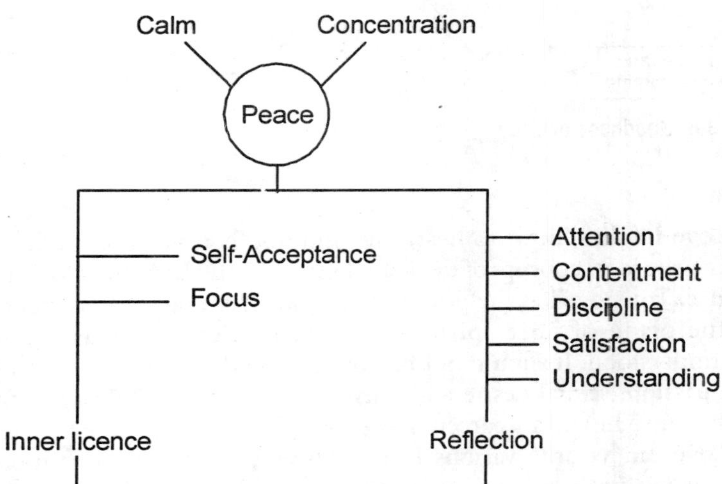

Fig. 3.3: Peace

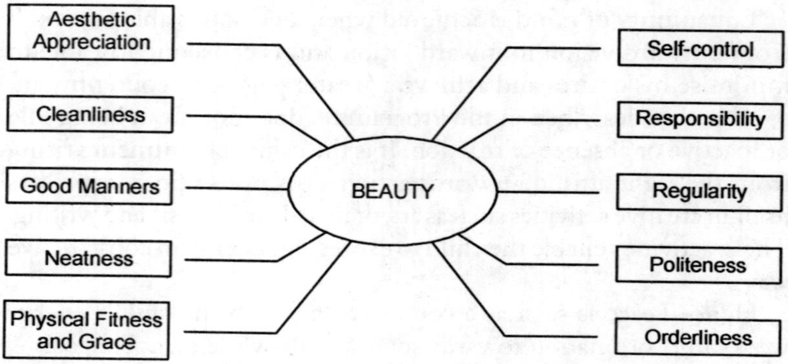

Fig. 3.4: Beauty

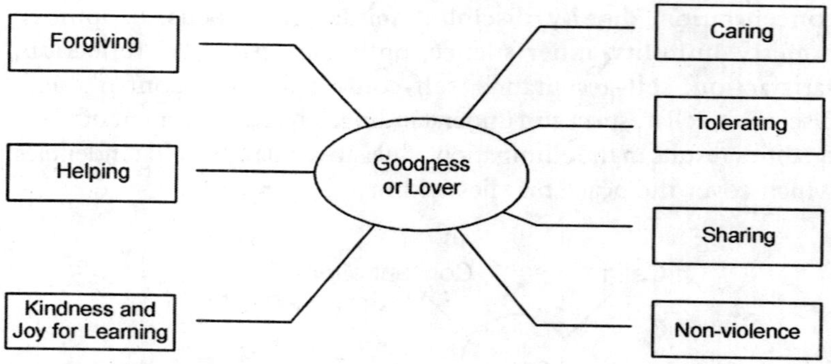

Fig. 3.4: Goodness or Love

Love

Love implies 'heart to heart ties' and not 'body-to-body affairs.' This is the ideal concept of the Four-letter 'LOVE.' Love has a 'divine' nature. True love has the power to take one from physical existence to the plane of pure spirit. However, it is often misused and misunderstood. It should not be mixed up with impurities of mind like passion, sexual desire and sensual gratification. Only a person with a pure heart can perceive true love.

Love can assume various forms. Usually worldly love is more concerned with 'taking' or 'possessing' rather than 'giving' and 'renouncing.' It is concerned with attachment, possessiveness, jealousy, sensuality and sexuality.

Love for fellow beings is considered sometimes even higher than love for Him (Almighty). It is said, "Those who live but do not love are as good as dead, even though they appear to be alive."

Divine love can be experienced only when the mind is 'still' (स्थिर) and we listen to our heart. The path of this kind of love is described by Bhakti Saints and 'Sufis' as the easiest, simplest, purest and smoothest way to 'Enlightenment' or 'Salvation.'

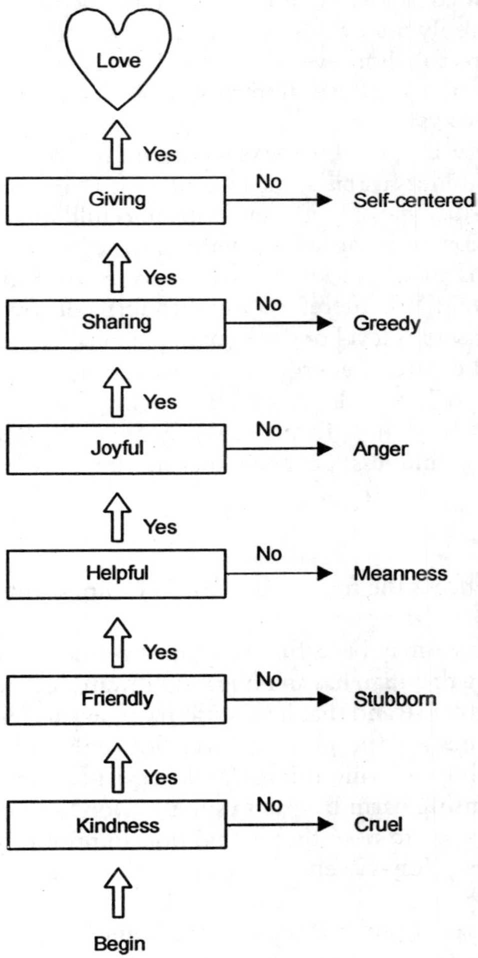

Fig. 3.5: Love

Within the context of the SSEHV programme the definition of Love is quite broad, encompassing feelings of reverence, affection, friendship, sympathy and compassion. It is love for all life form.

Love as a basic human value is conceived as much more than an emotion. Emotions have a tendency to be erratic.

Love is explained as a form of energy which each person transmits and receives every moment.

It is described as love "that flows from the depths of our soul."

It is not simply mercy or gentleness; it flows all the time and not just to persons to whom we are attached. It is for everyone, for the whole of creation. It affects all forms of life. The more it is shared, the more it grows.

The SSEHV Programme seeks to expand the vision of the child, thereby expanding his circle of love until it illumines all without distinction. This type of love transforms the child into a kind, caring and compassionate being who is willing to serve others and make sacrifices. It is unselfish love which is given unconditionally and indiscriminately. It is therefore a higher form of love. It develops the super-conscious level of the human personality—this being the psychological centre of energy in a human being.

Sub-values of love in the Programme include: caring, compassion, dedication, friendship, forgiveness, generosity, helping, inner happiness, joy, kindness, patience, sharing, sincerity, sympathy and tolerance.

Non-violence

Non-violence is the fruit of all the other values and our legacy to future generations.

Non-violence may be defined as "universal love." It fosters the understanding that man has an obligation towards every component part of this universe and that he should try to expand his love to all.

Non-violence goes beyond man's relation with his fellow-beings, it embraces all non-living things. With regard to human beings, it means not causing harm by one's thought, word and deed.

It is interesting to note that in addition to promoting the other human values, Non-violence represents the fruition of all these values.

That is to say, if one practises Truth, Right Conduct, Peace and Love, one is non-violent in one's actions.

Non-violence is described as the zenith of human achievement and perfection. It becomes a reality only when one recognises the oneness and unity of all creation. Then there is respect for all beings regardless of colour, class, occupation, religion or nationality. It gives rise to feelings of brotherhood, harmony, understanding and appreciation of other cultures and peoples.

In the context of plants and animals, non-violence means desisting from avoidable harm. It means non-violation of the law and balance of nature so that care of the environment, anti-pollution, preservation of plant and animal life, and preservation of nature becomes critical issues.

As far as non-living things go, non-violence incorporates care of and respect for the property and belongings of others and of the state. As a result, civic-mindedness, citizenship and the common good are impoıtant values.

Sub-values of Non-violence are compassion, concern for all life, consideration, cooperation, forgiveness, good manners, loyalty, universal love, unwillingness to hurt, appreciation of other cultures and religions, brotherhood, citizenship, equality, national awareness, respect for property, service to others, social justice and unity. Non-violence develops the spiritual level of the child's personality.

NOBLE SENTIMENTS ABOUT TRUTH AND PHILOSOPHICAL ANALYSIS OF TRUTH

Noble sentiments about truth have been expressed. Says an ancient aphorism, "Truth alone triumphs" (*Satyameva Jayate*). 'Satyam' (*Truth*), 'Shivam' (*Goodness*) and 'Sundaram' (*Beauty*) constitute the 'Trinity' of the ultimate values according to Indian philosophical thought. Gandhiji equated truth with God. 'God is Truth and Truth is God.'

Philosophical Analysis of Truth

Mahatma Buddha has said, "Believe nothing merely because you have been told it or because you yourself have imagined it.

Do not believe what you preceptor tells you merely out of respect for the teacher.

But whatever after due examination and analysis you find to be conducive to the good, the benefit, the welfare of all beings, that doctrine believe and cling to, and take it as your guide.

How to Arrive at Truth

Swami Dayananda (A.D. 1825–1883) advises us that the truth of everything that is learnt or taught should be carefully examined by the following five tests:

(i) *The Veda and Nature of God* – All that conforms to the teachings of the Vedas, nature and attributes and characteristics of God is right, the reverse is wrong.

(ii) *Laws of Nature* – All that tallies with the laws of nature is true, the reverse untrue, e.g., the statement that a child is born without the sexual union of its parents, being opposed to the laws of nature, can never be true.

(iii) *The practice and teachings of Aptas*, i.e., pious truthful, unprejudiced, honest, and learned men. All that is unopposed to their practice and teaching is acceptable, and the reverse is unacceptable.

(iv) *The Purity and Conviction of One's Own Soul* – What is good for you, is good for the world; what is painful to you, is painful to others. This ought to be the guiding principle of one's conduct towards others.

(v) *Eight kinds of Evidence*, viz., (1) Direct Cognisance, (2) Inference, (3) Analogy, (4) Testimony, (5) History, (6) Deduction, (7) Possibility, (8) Non-existence or Negation.

1. *Direct Cognisance* (*Pratyaksha*) is that knowledge which is the result of direct contract of the five senses with their objects, of the mind (faculty or organ of Attention) with the senses and of the soul with the mind.
2. *Anumona* (Inference). Literally it means that which follows direct cognisance. Two things have been observed to exist together at sometime and place, when on some other occasion, one of the two is observed, the other i.e., the unknown can be inferred.

   It is not true that wherever there is no fall in barometer although, the pressure may have been decreased. The mercury, through rise of temperature, expands and becomes lighter. Had the same pressure continued, the column of mercury would have risen higher up, but the fall of pressure compensated for the rise and left the mercury apparently where it was. The three canons of Kashyap, therefore, conclusively proved that the fall of the barometer is not the *linga* of the decrease of the pressure. Similar reasoning will show that the decrease in the weight of the super incumbent column of mercury is the *linga* (inference) of the decrease of pressure.

Inference is of three kinds:

(a) *Purvavat* is one, in which you reason from cause to effect, e.g., the inference of coming rain from the sight of clouds; or, again, you see a wedding, you naturally infer that some day the wedded couple will have children. Or, again you see students engaged in the pursuit of knowledge, and you infer that some day they will become men of learning.

(b) *Sheshavat* inference is one, in which you reason from effects to causes.

Examples: You see a flood in the river, and infer that it must have rained on the mountain from which the river issues. Again, you see a child, you at once infer that the child must have had a father. Again, you see this world, and infer the existence of the Spiritual cause—the elementary matter. Or, again, take another example. When you see a man in pleasure or pain, you at once infer that he must have done a virtuous or sinful deed before, since you have noticed that the consequence of a sinful act is pain, and that of a virtuous deed, pleasure.

(c) *Samanyatodrishta* is that kind of inference in which there is no relation of cause and effect between the known datum and the thing to be inferred, but there is some kind of similarity between the two; for example, you know that no one can get to another place without moving from the first and hence if you find a person in a certain place, you can easily infer that he must have come to the latter place by moving from the first.

3. *Upamana* (Analogy) is the knowledge of a thing from its likeness to another. The thing which is required to be known is called *Sadhya*, and that which becomes the means of this knowledge from one kind of likeness between the two is called *Sadhana*.

   Examples: A man says to his servant: "Go and fetch Vishnu Mittra." The latter answers that he does not know him, as he had never seen him before. Thereupon the master says: "You know Deva Datta, don't you?" Upon the servant's answering in the affirmative, his master continues "Well, Vishnu Mittra is just like Deva Datta." So the servant went out to find Vishnu Mittra. As he was passing through a street, he saw a man very much like Deva Datta, and thought that man must be Vishnu Mittra, and forthwith brought him to his master. Or, take another example; you want to know what a Yak is. Well, someone tells you, it is just like an ox. Next time you go to a jungle, you happen to see an animal very much like an ox, you at once know that it is the Yak, you asked your friend about. Now this kind of knowledge, i.e., knowledge of Vishnu Mittra, from his likeness to Deva Datta, and of Yak from its likeness to an ox is called *Upamana* or knowledge by Analogy. The words Vishnu Mittra and Yak are called *Sadhya*, whilst Deva Datta and ox *Sadhana*, in the above two instances.

4. *Shabda* (Testimony, literally word): The word of an '*Apt*' is called '*Shabda*.'

   An *Apt* is a person who is a thorough scholar, well-versed in all the sciences and philosophies, physical and spiritual, is virtuous, truthful, active, free from passions and desires, imbued with love for others, and who is an altruistic teacher of humanity, solely actuated with the desire of benefiting the world by his knowledge, experience and convictions. God being the truest and greatest of all *Aptas*, His word, the Veda, is also included in *Shabda* (Testimony).
5. *Itihas* is that which tells us that such and such a person was so and so, he did such and such a thing. In other words, *Itihas* is the History of a country or the biography of a person. (The experience of the past recorded in history can be applied to solve many a difficult question of the day.)
6. *Arthapatti* (Conclusion or Deduction): It is a conclusion which naturally follows from the statement of a fact; for instance, one says to another: "Rain falls from clouds" or "an effect follows a cause." The natural conclusion that can be drawn from the above statement is: "There can be no rain when there are no clouds," or "no effect follows when a cause does not exist."
7. *Sambhava* (Possibility): When you hear a thing, the first thing that enters your mind is whether such and such a thing is

possible. Anything that runs counter to the laws of nature is not possible, and hence it can never be true; for example, if you are told that a child was born without parents, such and such a person raised the dead to life gain, or made stones float on the sea, lifted mountains, broke the moon into pieces, was God incarnate, or saw horns on the head of a man, or married a couple born of sterile mothers. You could at once know that it could not have possibly happened, being opposed to the laws of Nature. That alone is possible which is in conformity with the laws of Nature.

8. *Abhava* (Absence or Negation): You infer the existence of a thing in some other place from its absence from the place where you were told you would find it; for instance, a gentleman said to his man: "Go and bring the elephant from the elephant-house." He went there but found that the elephant was not there. He naturally concluded that he must be somewhere near about. So he went out and looked about for the elephant and found him not very far from its proper place and brought him to his master.

These eight kinds of evidence have been briefly described. Their number can be reduced to four if History be included under Testimony, and Deduction, Possibility and Negation under inference.

Six Kinds of Inferential Knowledge

There are six kinds of inferential knowledge, i.e., knowledge derived from the relation of a sign with the object signified:

1. That in which we proceed from causes to effects.
   Example: A man at some distance sees a man, claps his hands; he at once infers that sound will be produced.
2. That in which we proceed from effects to causes. (*Vaisheshika* IX. 2. I.)
   Example: A person hears the sound (peculiar to the clapping of hands), he at once infers that there has been clapping of hands closeby.
3. *Samyogi* (Concurrent) knowledge is that which is obtained from the concurrence of one thing with another.
   Example: The mention of the word body at once suggests the existence of skin along with it.
4. *Samvayi* (Inherent) knowledge is that which is obtained from

the inference of something (i.e., an attribute substance or an action) in another.
Example: We know Extension inheres in Ether, therefore, from the mere mention of the word Ether, Extension is at once inferred.

5. *Ekartha Samvayi* (Knowledge). When two things (such as attributes) reside in substances, the knowledge of one at once suggests the other. This kind of inferential knowledge is called *Ekartha Samvayi*.
   Example: We see the orange colour of an orange and at once infer that it must be smooth to touch or sweet in taste.
6. *Virodhi* (Antithetic) knowledge is that which is gained from the natural opposition of ideas or things.
   Example: White colour suggests black colour; sweet taste suggests bitter taste; hissing of a snake at once suggests that its natural foe, such as a mongoose, must be closeby.

Source: Biswas Anand, Aggarwal, J.C. '*Seven Indian Educationists*.' Arya Books, New Delhi, 2004.

NON-VIOLENCE AND TRUTH WITH SPECIAL REFERENCE TO GANDHIJI

The concept of non-violence was popularised by Buddhism and Jainism. Here the relationship between non-violence and truth as explained by Gandhiji in his work entitled "*Non-Violence: Weapon of the Brave*" is given.

Gandhiji's Return from South Africa with New Ideology: 'Ahimsa' and 'Satyagraha'

For about two decades in South Africa (1894–1914), Gandhiji waged his struggle against the discriminatory and humiliating laws of the African Government through '*Ahimsa*' and '*Satyagraha*.' With these two weapons, he combated with the British rulers in India. The masses of India followed him very faithfully and sincerely whenever he launched his non-violent movements against the brutal force of the rulers.

Ahimsa (Non-violence)

Gandhiji does not agree with the literal meaning of '*Ahimsa*,' which means non-killing. "'*Ahimsa*' really means that you may not offend anybody, you may not harbour an uncharitable thought even in connection with one who may consider himself to be your enemy." Again he says, "Non-violence is the quality of heart."

Gandhiji gave so much importance to *Ahimsa* that he said, "*Ahimsa* is the rule and breath of my life."

"The principle of '*Ahimsa*' is hurt by every evil thought, by undue haste, by lying, by hatred, by wishing ill of anybody."

His '*Mantra*' regarding '*Ahimsa*' is, "Truth exists, it alone exists. It is the only God and there is but one way of realising it; there is but one means and that is '*Ahimsa*.'"

In the words of Gandhiji, "*Ahimsa* and truth are so intertwined that it is practically impossible to disentangle and separate them. They are like the two sides of the coin. Who can say which is the obverse and which is the reverse? Nevertheless '*Ahimsa*' is the means and truth is the end."

Non-violence according to Gandhiji "does not mean submission to the will of the evil doer, but it means the putting one's whole soul against the will of the tyrant."

To Gandhiji, "The jewel of non-violence was discovered during the search for and contemplation of truth."

Gandhiji considered the following requisites for practising '*Ahimsa*':

(i) Truth
(ii) Purity of heart
(iii) Fearlessness
(iv) Freedom from greed
(v) Honesty of purpose.

Satyagraha

The word '*Satyagraha*' is composed of two words i.e., '*Satya*' (truth) and '*agraha*' (holding fast). It means 'holding on truth' no matter what happens. It implies 'Truth force" i.e., truth is force, a power or a weapon. The term was coined in South Africa and Gandhiji himself described it as 'Passive Resistance,' but later on he made a distinction between the two ideas. "'*Satyagraha*' differs from 'Passive Resistance.' The latter Passive Resistance has been conceived as a weapon of the weak and does not exclude the use of physical force or violence for the purpose of gaining one's objective or end. The former i.e., '*Satyagraha*' is conceived as a weapon of the strongest who is truthful and it excludes the use of violence in any shape or form."

Regarding, '*Satyagraha*' Gandhiji says, '*Satyagraha*' is the law of love for all. It eschews violence absolutely.

Gandhiji has identified 'truth' and 'non-violence' as the most important values or the two central pillars to ensure peace, perfection in thought and deed of every individual, progress and prosperity.

Violence is the weapon of the weak;
Non-violence; that of the strong

★

He who has neither peace nor strength
Of mind, how can he have knowledge?

★

Pure love removes all weariness
Without truth it is impossible to observe

★

Any principles or rules in life.
There must be truth in thought.
Truth in speech and Truth in action.

Mahatma Gandhi

NON-VIOLENCE AS EXPLAINED BY MAHATMA GANDHI

Ten Questions asked by a correspondent and the Answers given by Gandhiji.

Q. 1 The first question is:

What is non-violence, an attitude of the mind or non-destruction of life? If it be the latter, is it possible to translate it into practice and carry it to its logical consequences when we destroy numberless lives daily in taking our meals, etc? We cannot even eat vegetables in that case.

Ans. Non-violence is both an attitude of mind and action consequent upon it. No doubt, there is life in vegetables. But the taking of vegetable life is inevitable. It is none the less destruction of life. Only it may be regarded as excusable.

Q. 2 The second question is:

If we cannot avoid destroying life, it certainly does not mean that we should recklessly destroy it; but then, in proved cases of necessity it cannot be objected to on principle. It may be objected to on expediency.

Ans. Even in proved cases of necessity, violence cannot be defended "on principle." It may be defended on grounds of expedience.

Q. 3 The third question is:

If non-violence is non-destruction of life, how can you consistently ask anybody to give up his own life in a cause however holy and righteous it may be? Would that not be violence to one's own self?

Ans. I can consistently ask a person to give up his life for a cause and yet not be guilty of violence. For non-violence means refraining from injury to others.

Q. 4 The fourth is:

It is human nature to love one's own life. If one should sacrifice one's life when necessary for his country and people, why should he not sacrifice the lives of others when necessary? We have only to prove whether it was necessary. It is, therefore, a matter of expediency again.

Ans. "He that shall love his own life shall lose it. He that shall lose his own life shall find it. "Sacrifice of the lives of others cannot be justified on grounds of necessity, for it is impossible to prove necessity. We may not be judges ourselves. The sole judges must be those whose lives we would take. One good reason for non-violence is our fallible judgment. The inquisitors implicitly believed in the righteousness of their deeds, but we now know that they were wholly wrong.

Q. 5 The fifth question is:

What is the differences between sacrifice and murder?

Ans. Sacrifice consists in suffering in one's own person so that others may benefit. Murder consists in making others suffer unto death so that the murderer, or those others for whom he murders, may benefit.

Q. 6 The sixth question is:

Is a doctor, who operates upon you, condemnable, for he is violent in giving you trouble temporarily? Do we not praise him all the more for that—looking not, to his violent action but to his attitude of mind which is to give relief to the patient?

Ans. This is a misuse of the word violence, which means causing injury to another without his consent or without doing any good to him. In my case, the surgeon caused me temporary pain.

Q. 7 His seventh question is:

Is not physical force as much a potent factor of life as any other force? As non-violence can be taken by cowards as a garb to cover their cowardice, so can violence be misused by brutes and tyrants. It does not prove that violence of itself is bad.

Ans. Physical force undoubtedly is a potent factor of life. Violence has certainly been misused by tyrants, but in the sense in which I have defined violence, its good use is inconceivable. See the definition in the answer to the preceding question.

Q. 8 The eighth question is:

You will put lunatics and dangerous criminals who are a nuisance to society in prisons. Will you allow us to capture those civilised criminals, who are functioning as government officials today, and deport or imprison them in some Himalayan caves instead of murdering them?

Ans. I am not sure that it is right to put lunatics or criminals, dangerous or otherwise, in prisons, i.e., for punishment. Lunatics are not so put even now. And we are reaching a time when even criminals will be put under restraint for their ultimate reform, not for their punishment. But I would gladly join any society for the confinement, under proper safeguards for their comfort, of the Viceroy and every civilian, English or Indian, who are today consciously or unconsciously bleeding India, provided that a scheme can be produced before me that is perfectly feasible from every point of view. And I would be prepared to join such a society even though it may be argued that such confinement might fall within my definition of violence.

Q. 9 The ninth question is:

What is more inhuman and terrible, rather what is more violent, to let 33 millions suffer, stagnate and perish, or a few thousand be killed? What would you prefer, to see the slow death of a mass of 33 millions. But then, it is a matter of detail and not principle. It may be later on discussed whether it is expedient or not. But if it is proved that by killing a few hundred, we can put a stop to the degeneration of 33 millions, will you object to violence on principle?

Ans. There is no principle worth the name if it is not wholly good. I swear by non-violence because I know that it alone conduces to the highest good of mankind, not merely in the next world but in this also. I object to violence because, when it appears to do good, the good is only temporary; the evil it does is permanent. I do not believe that the killing of every Englishman can do the slightest good to India. The millions will be just as badly off as they are today, if someone made it possible to kill off every Englishman tomorrow. The responsibility is more ours than that of the English for the present state of things. The English will be powerless to do evil if we will but do good. Hence my incessant emphasis on reform from within.

But, before the revolutionary, I have urged non-violence not on the highest ground of morality but on the lower ground of expedience. I contend that the revolutionary method cannot succeed in India. If an open warfare were a possibility, I may concede that we may tread the path of violence that the other countries have and at least evolve the qualities that bravery on the battlefield brings forth. But attainment of *swaraj* through warfare I hold to be an impossibility for anytime that we can foresee. Warfare may give us another rule for the English rule but not self-rule in terms of the masses. The pilgrimage to *swaraj* is a painful climb. It requires attention to details. It means vast organising ability, it means penetration into the villages solely for the service of the villagers. In other words, it means national education, i.e., education of the masses. It means an awakening of national consciousness among the masses. It will not spring like the magician's mango. It will grow almost unperceived like the banyan tree. A bloody revolution will never perform the trick. Haste here is most certainty waste. The revolution of the spinning-wheel is the quickest revolution conceivable.

Q. 10 The tenth and the last question is:

Is not all logic and reason discarded where vital interests of life are concerned? Is it not a fact that a few selfish, tyrant and obdurate men may, as they do, refuse to listen to reason and continue to rule tyrannise and do injustice to a mass of people? Lord Krishna failed to bring about a settlement peacefully between the obdurate Kauravas and the Pandavas. *Mahabharata* may be fiction. Poor Krishna may be less spiritual. But even you failed to persuade your judge to resign from his post and not convict you, whom even he, as everybody else, regarded innocent. How far can persuasion through self-sacrifice be successful in such cases?

Ans. It is sad but true that, where so-called vital interests are concerned, logic and reason are thrown to the wind. Tyrants are, indeed, obdurate. The English tyrant is obduracy personified. But he is a multi-headed monster. He refuses to be killed. He cannot be paid in his own coin, for he has left none for us to pay him with. I have a coin that is not cast in his mint and he cannot steal it. It is superior to any he has yet produced. It is non-violence; and the symbol of it is spinning-wheel. I have, therefore, presented it to country with fullest confidence. Krishna failed to do nothing he wished to do, so says the author of the *Mahabharata*. He was omnipotent. It is futile to drag Krishna from His heights. If He has to be judged as a mere mortal, I fear He will fare badly and will have to take a back seat. *Mahabharata* is neither fiction nor history commonly so-called. It is the history of the human soul in which God as Krishna is the chief actor. There are many things in that poem that my poor understanding cannot fathom. There are in it many things which are obvious interpolations. It is not a treasure chest. It is a mine which needs to be explored, which needs to be dug deep and from which diamonds have to be extracted after removing much foreign matter. Therefore, I would urge my friends, the full-fledged revolutionaries, or those in the making, or on the verge of being such, to keep their feet firm on mother earth and not scale the Himalayan heights to which the poet took Arjuna and his other heroes. Anyway, I must respectfully refuse even to attempt the ascent. The plains of Hindustan are good enough for me.

Source: *Non-violence*: *Weapon of the Brave*, M.K. Gandhi, Navjivan Trust.

4

Value Development and Education: Approaches and Strategies

NPE ON THE ROLE OF EDUCATION IN VALUE DEVELOPMENT

National Policy on Education 1986, in Part VIII, Para 8.5 has made following observations:

- "In our culturally plural society, education should foster eternal values, oriented towards the unity and integration of our people."
- "....value education has a profound positive content, based on our heritage, national goals, universal perceptions."

In Part XII under the heading "The future" NPE (1986) has further observed that

- The future shape of education in India is too complex to envision with precision. Yet, given our tradition which always put a high premium on intellectual and spiritual attainment we are bound to succeed in achieving our objective.

The Programme of Action on National Policy on Education 1986 in the chapter entitled "The Cultural Perspective" under sub-heading 'Institutes of Moral Education' has made the following observations:

"A special place has been assigned to imparting of value oriented education in the Education Policy document. A beginning would be made by instituting a special study on value oriented education. Based on its analysis, it would in collaboration with NCERT and state institutions, help in suggesting broad parameters of values of integrity, truth, devotion, loyalty etc., with particular reference to their embodiment in Indian heritage, so as to blend naturally with the overall educational process" (p. 176).

CONCEPTUAL FRAMEWORK FOR VALUE DEVELOPMENT

Principal A.R. Seetha Ram (B.Ed. Section) of the Ramakrishna Institute of Moral and Spiritual Education, Mysore has suggested the following conceptual framework for value education.

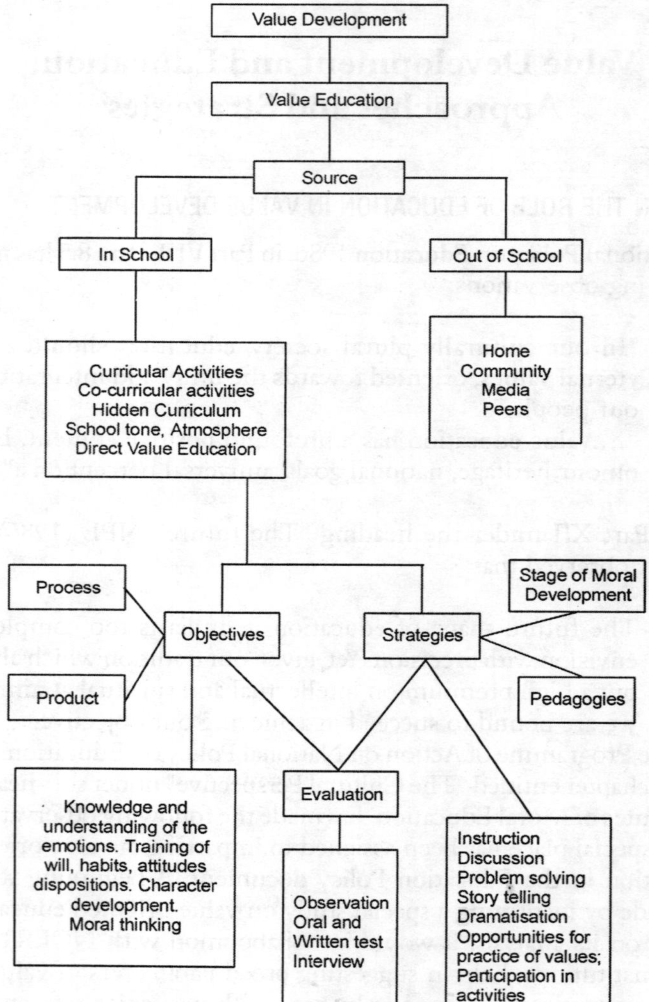

Fig. 4.1: A Schematic Representation of the Process of Value education

Source: National Seminar on 'Philosophy of Value Orinted Education 'Theory and Practice.' January 18–20, 2002, New Delhi.

According to Marmar Mukhopadhyay of NIEPA, Value development takes place as shown in the following Fig. 4.2:

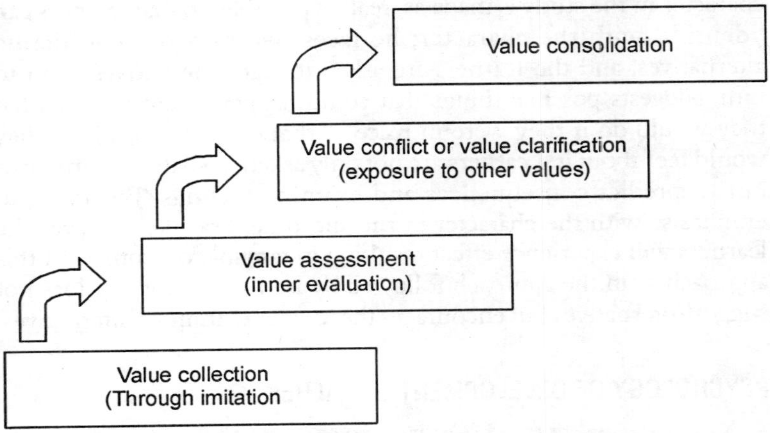

Fig. 4.2: Stages of Value Development

The human behaviour is determined by the consolidated values. It is the consolidated values that provides predictability of human behaviour; and indeed, the very foundation of the personality that has been described as the style of the man/woman. (National Seminar-cum-Workshop on 'Education in Human Values and Life Skills in Higher Education,' (NIEPA–May 24, 2001)

VALUE-DEVELOPMENT STRATEGY SUGGESTED BY J.R. FRAENKEL (1969)

Fraenkel believes that since values are learned, schools should be concerned with how they are learned by the learners—accidentally or as planned. He concentrates on the question what values do we want in our learners and how they can be developed. Accordingly in teaching values, it becomes necessary to define more accurately and precisely what is meant by an value and how an accepted value might be seen in actual behaviour. Fraenkel cites the following example as to how a given value 'dignity and worth of others' may be manifested as under:

'Waits' until others have finished speaking before speaking himself' (does not interrupt others) and

'Encourages' everyone else in a discussion to offer his opinion (does not monopolise the conversation), etc.

In this 'Value-developing strategy' certain instructional objectives are used to present an anecdote for the learner's consideration. The character in the study is made as 'real' as possible, so that learners can 'identify' with the character; he faces two or more conflicting alternatives, and the learners are asked to state alternatives open to him, suggests possible things that could happen to him, state what they would do if they were in place of that character and how they would feel about it. Learners are not only asked to analyse alternatives but to predict consequences and examine feelings. By trying to emphasise with the character in the anecdote, Fraenkel believes the learners will experience effect resulting in tangible outcomes. In this approach as in the approach followed by Raths, the teacher does not suggest alternatives but encourages the learner to think of alternatives.

PSYCHOLOGY OF DEVELOPMENT OF VALUES

According to Hipple, T.W. (1969), "Values are conscious, unconscious motivators and justifiers of the actions and judgement."

Dr. Lalit Kishore, in his publication '*Value-Oriented Education*' (1990) has summarised the views of R. Safaya given in '*Human Values and Education*' (1986) on the development of values as under in the form of Table.

Technique	Description
1. Precept – ideal	Presentation of the ideal behaviours of parents and teachers.
2. Influence	Use of approval and disapproval of acts, humour.
3. Identification	Identification with a child hero from a story, novel, scripture or identification with a desirable group or individual.
4. Association and Conditioning	Creating situations of enjoyment: Satisfaction in various co-curricular and curricular programmes.
5. Ventilation	Providing an outlet through verbal and written statements on controversial issues.
6. Parable and Allogory	Short stories, songs, poems, depicting healthy attitudes.
7. Psycho-drama	Creating artificial situations to affect children's mind positively.
8. Role-playing and Socio-Drama	Acting out certain situations by taking various roles and looking at solutions of value problems.

PROCESS OF VALUE-ORIENTATION

Prof. J.S. Rajput has observed that value orientation is a gradual process which starts with value awareness followed by value clarification/appraisal. It then leads to value selection which generates value commitment. Value commitment leads to value action. Value commitment has to be reaffirmed over and over again, so that value erosion or dilution does not take place. The ever-evolving circles of value education are graphically presented by Prof. J.S. Rajput as shown in the Fig. 4.3.

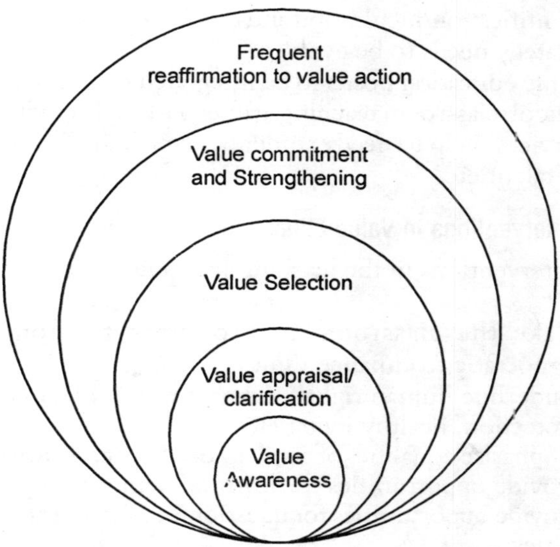

Fig. 4.3: Ever Evolving circles of Value Education

Source: *'Journal of Value Education,'* July 2003, NCERT.

NCERT APPROACH TO VALUE EDUCATION

J.S. Rajput, Director, NCERT in NCERT presentation at the National Seminar on the theme of "Philosophy of Value-Oriented Education: Theory and Practice" (January 18–20, 2002), organised by Indian Council of Philosophical Research, New Delhi, summarised the NCERT approach to value education. Its salient features are:

1. Value education and education about religions should not form a separate subject of study for examination at any stage.
2. These would be so judiciously integrated with all subjects of study in the scholastic areas that the objectives thereof would be directly and indirectly achieved in the classroom, at the school assembly places, playgrounds, cultural centres and other rich places.
3. Every teacher has to be a teacher of values.
4. Every activity, unit, textbooks and classroom interaction should be examined from the point of view of value identification/inculcation and reinforcement and appropriate strategy needs to be evolved.
5. Value education needs to be integrated to all activities of the school, classroom teaching, games, cultural activities, welfare services, help to needy students, remediation and nurturing of talent etc.

General Interventions in Value Education

The Interventions in the teaching-learning process must:

1. Make the classroom environment tension free and democratic to enhance values.
2. Underline human rights, rights of the child, environmental protection, healthy living etc.
3. Emphasise equalities of gender, social caste, class and religion.
4. Provide opportunities for learning democratic principles.
5. Provide opportunities for questioning, sharing and practising values.
6. Highlight the values inherent in different subject areas.
7. Encourage exhibitions, Bal-melas, Fairs and folk cultural activities.
8. Provide appropriate guidance and counselling.
9. Organise inter-state cultural exchange programme.

Stage Specific Inputs

The examplar activities at different stages are highlighted below:

At Elementary Stage

- The school assembly, group singing, practising silence and meditation.
- Simple and interesting stories about the lives and teaching

of prophets, saints and sacred texts of different religions.
- Field activities like game and sports, social work leading to the attitude of service (*seva*) to humanity and other creatures, and even to nature.
- Cultural activities, plays etc., on appropriate theme.

At the Secondary/Higher Secondary Stages

- Morning assembly, readings from books of wisdom, great literature or an appropriate address by a teacher or a guest speaker.
- Essential teachings of major world religions, comparative study of the philosophy of religion.
- Social service during holidays outside school hours.
- Community singing programmes, National Integration Camps, the National Social Service, Nation Cadet Corps, Scouts' and Guides programme.
- Cultural activities, play, debates etc., on appropriate themes.

School may organise joint celebrations of the important occasions and festivals of major religious and cultural groups.

Role of Teachers

The criticality of the role of teachers is well established and widely acknowledged. They have to be professionally prepared and made to internalise their role in value inculcation. Since every teacher is a value educator, it is expected that he/she:

- Would develop a clear vision of his role in value orientation.
- Would be able to identify the potential of different subjects and situations in school for fostering universal human values and be sensitised about his own influence as role models.
- Would be able to analyse his own biases and attitude towards students.
- Would evolve a positive approach to authentic orientation related to different religions and religion related values.
- Would be a good communicator.
- Would be able to delineate stage specific strategies.

Source: National Seminar, 2002.

STRATEGIES FOR VALUE-ORIENTATION

Several educators in general do not favour teaching of human values as a separate subject of study. However, some educators have developed some strategies for imparting values in the formal as well as informal settings. Important strategies of value-orientation are:

1. Attitude Development Strategy
2. Case Study Strategy
3. Critical Inquiry Approach
4. Experimental Approach Strategy
5. Role-Pay Strategy
6. Total Atmosphere Strategy
7. Value Clarification Strategy
8. Value Sheet Strategy.

Critical Inquiry Approach. Critical inquiry approach aims at helping people discover what is right through constant critical inquiry. The main idea is to harness their inherent energies for the pursuit of sound values.

The Total Atmospheric Approach. In this approach attempts are made to impart values through the use of activities, experiences and exercises that habituate children in the right mode of conduct thus strengthening their character.

The Integrated Approach. This approach combines the above mentioned approaches. It aims at providing training in inculcating values through all types of programmes. The teacher integrates the relevant values in the daily lessons as well in other activities outside the classroom. Thus the integrated approach is followed both through curricular and co-curricular activities.

VALUE CLARIFICATION

Origin and Meaning of the Concept Value Clarification

The concept of value clarification was coinced by L.E. Raths, M.F. Harmin and S.B. Simon in 1966. Value clarification strategy is an attempt at explaining the process of acquisition of values of children. According to the authors of this concept, this strategy has important implications for teachers for facilitating and structuring the learning situations relating to values.

The originators of this concept believe that a value must be freely chosen. Such choice implies that alternatives must be explored. Learners should be provided freedom of choice and they should be permitted to live with the choices.

The teacher may adopt one or more of the several ways to assist the learners clarify their values. In this context it is pertinent to note that many learners do not clearly know what values they have, what values they need to acquire and are confused. As a result, in the absence of any effective guidance, some learners may become apathetic and frustrated.

The primary aim is to let them examine alternatives to project the consequences of the position they take, and to decide how they feel about a given issue. They may then be encouraged to act in terms of their chosen values.

One such technique is "informal encounter with learners." A teacher following this strategy may raise a passing question to a learner's expressed feelings about something. For example, if a learner, at the verge of deciding his future courses of study expresses a desire to study Commerce, the teacher may help him consider how strongly, he feels that way, whether he knows about other possibilities, and what reasons he has for his decision, and so on. This will stimulate the learner to think through his decisions before he implements them.

Some other strategies such as use of anecdotes to represent certain values to elicit learner's reactions, 'value sheets' asking learner to arrange values in a hierarchy, role-playing to explore the extent of identification one feels with character or idea etc., can be useful in this regard.

Environment Needed for Value Clarification

The use of value clarification techniques demands a psychologically safe classroom in which learners feel free to hold values that may be different from those of other learners or of the teacher. Rogers' Client-Centred approach which advocates genuine respect for the learner and his views seems useful as an implementation strategy. The classroom atmosphere is non-threatening and trust is built-up between teacher and the learner. The teacher should not feel otherwise in case of disagreement and will be tolerant and non-coercive.

ROLE-PLAY TECHNIQUE IN VALUE EDUCATION

Students generally take pleasure in playing the role of other persons. This technique is basically a socio-drama technique. It provides an ideal setting for highlighting values.

According to K.H. Hoover (1976), role-play has the following advantages:

1. The enactment of selected situations provides a valuable opportunity for discussion of actual feeling reactions.
2. To live for a short while in the shadow of another person offers a significant opportunity for insight into other person's feelings.
3. A stimulation of reality may be superior to reality itself for instructional purposes.
4. The feelings often concealed in real life come forth during the role playing sessions.
5. The technique provides the learner with new insights into possible responses to social situations.
6. An analysis of the dramatised situation stresses factors which contribute to actual feeling reactions.
7. Role-playing technique combines the joy of acting with learning.

The procedure for the role-playing technique is illustrated in the following flow-chart:

Observation and analysis by students

↑

Enactment of the situation

↑

Briefing the role-player about situation and roles

↑

Selection of roles

↑

Developing the situation

↑

Identification of the problem

Fig. 4.4: Procedure of Flow-chart of Role-Play Technique

ROLE REVERSAL IN VALUE DEVELOPMENT

Role reversal consists of asking the learner to play the role of another person whose views are dissimilar to his own. The learner is, thereby, involved in a more realistic situation than simple discussion. He is able to get the feel of how he and others are behaving and why they behave in those ways. The situation may be contrived or it may develop informally. For example, for giving the learner an understanding of how a child who has some physical handicap or a child with limited financial resources at home feels, the teacher may evolve certain themes concentrating around such learners and ask them without such limitations to take on their roles and interact. Learners will then learn values like 'dignity of individuals' in their own right, 'non-discrimination' etc. An imaginative and creative teacher can deal with attitudes and prejudices in a meaningful manner, involving the learners not merely at intellectual level but also tapping their emotional resources.

KOHLBERG'S MORAL DEVELOPMENT STAGES

Kohlberg (1971) who was influenced by John Dewey and Jean Piaget, postulated cognitive developmental series of stages of moral development. According to him the stages follow the same order in all the children but the rate at which they will attain mastery of various stages may vary. Also, one cannot teach a higher stage the child is ready for, but when the child is ready, one can help stimulate him to move to the next higher stage. Kohlberg believes that we should stimulate children to move to higher moral stages, arguing that this is constitutional, philosophically justified, and socially useful (Kohlberg and Turiel, 1971). While it is recognised that various cultures may carry out moral values in different way, their ultimate values are usually considered to be similar. The school should, therefore, aim at helping children to move from lower moral orientation to higher. Kohlberg's moral stages include the progress of the child from pre-conventional level where the child is responsive to cultural rules because of fear of punishment through conventional level where the attitude is that of 'conformity' to social order perceived as valuable in its own right to the post-conventional autonomous stage where the moral values and principles have validity apart from authority.

VALUE CRISIS AND ROLE OF EDUCATION

Value crisis in a society implies the erosion of traditional values of society or situation of dilemma when there is little balance between traditional values and modem values. There is lack of synthesis. Material values override the ethical, moral, social and spiritual values.

At present, India is passing through a period of value crisis in several fields of national life. It is generally being said that the life of individuals as well as our social life is plagued with the evil values of corruption, cynicism, disparity, disruption, hypocrisy and violence.

It is very unfortunate that our role-models i.e., leaders of various shades fail to inspire us to pursue higher values of life.

Several conflicting ideologies are also at work. On the one hand, there is the value crisis of Indianisation and on the other hand value-crisis on account of overemphasis on modernisation and westernisation.

The Education Commission 1964–66 has observed, "We believe that India should strive to bring science and the values of the spirit together in harmony and thereby pave their way for the eventual emergence of a society which would cater to the needs of the whole man and not only to a particular fragment of his personality."

Areas of Value Crisis

1. Modern emphasis on Democratic Values as against traditional Colonial Values.
2. Modern emphasis on Socialist Values as against the traditional emphasis on Capitalist Values.
3. Modern emphasis on Secular Values as against traditional emphasis on Religious Values.
4. Modern emphasis on Scientific Values as against traditional emphasis on Superstitious Values.
5. Modern emphasis on Global Values as against Traditional emphasis on Nationalist Values.
6. Modern emphasis on Emotional Integration and National Unity as against the traditional emphasis on Local/Regional Values.

Synthesis Between the Traditional Values and Modern Values: Synthesis Between Scientific, Secular and Spiritual Values

In our attempt to inculcate values through education, we should draw freely upon our own traditions as well as the traditions of other countries and cultures of the world. There are strands within Indian thought itself which can lead to the new outlook appropriate for a modern society, and which can prepare the people for a willing acceptance of life.

Role of Education in Value Crisis. The National Policy on Education

(1986 and as amended in 1992) observes, "Every country develops its system of education to express and promote its unique socio-cultural identity and also to meet the challenges of the times. There are moments in history when a new direction has to be given to an aged-old process. That moment is today."

NPE has further observed, "Education has an acculturating role. It refines sensitivities and perceptions."

Readjustment in the Curriculum. The NPE has expressed its concern over Value Crisis and the role of education as, "The growing concern over the erosion of essential values and an increasing cynicism in society has brought to focus the need for readjustments in the curriculum in order to make education a forceful tool for the cultivation of social and moral values."

Value-based Curriculum in India

Value-based curriculum is the need of the hour to overcome value-crisis. It should take note of the following points and accordingly include appropriate contents.

1. Pluralist nature of our society comprising multi-linguistic, multi-racial and multi-religious groups.
2. Existence of a sizeable section of the society below the poverty line.
3. Deep-rooted superstitions of people.
4. Fatalistic attitude.
5. Increased use of 'money power' in democratic elections.
6. Widespread prevalence of corruption.
7. Consumer culture or materialistic outlook.
8. Growth of favouritism.

School Programme for Developing Values of Various Kinds

Following are the important activities to be undertaken in the school in this regard:

1. Celebration of national festivals
2. Social service programmes
3. Emphasis on the unity of all religions, harmony among communities and national integration
4. Development of scientific temper
5. Community prayer in the school

6. Health and cleanliness programmes
7. Socially useful productive programmes
8. Citizenship training programmes
9. Cultural and recreational programmes
10. Student self-government in schools
11. Introduction of Information Technology
12. International understanding
13. Appropriate teaching-learning situations

Role of the Teacher

The teachers must play an important role in such programmes. The most important aspect is that they should set good examples of conduct and behaviour which the students may imbibe in themselves.

It may be stressed that the teachers, the educational workers, the educators, the supervisors, the administrators and above all the parents must try their best to promote value-oriented education.

Summing up: India is on the move again with the promise of new renaissance in the making. The most powerful tool in the process of this renaissance and modernisation is education based on secular values on the one hand and on the other on science and technology. In this context we cannot do better than to quote Pt. Jawaharlal Nehru, "Can we combine the progress of science and technology with the progress of mind and spirit also? We cannot be untrue to science because that represents the basic fact of life today. Still less can we be untrue to those essential principles for which India has stood in the past throughout the ages. Let us then pursue our path to industrial progress with our strength and vigour and at the same time remember that material riches without toleration and compassion and wisdom may well turn to dust and ashes."

5

Sources of Values

IMPORTANT SOURCES OF VALUES

Among the important sources of values, following deserve careful treatment:

1. Culture as a source of values.
2. Religio-spiritual source of values.
3. Constitution as a source of value.

CULTURE AS A SOURCE OF VALUE

The term culture is used in different senses and this has resulted in a good deal of confusion. Here a few definitions of culture are given to throw light in its various dimensions.

1. According to Arnold, "Culture looks beyond machinery ...Culture has one great passion—the passion for sweetness and light."
2. In the words of Bogardus, "Culture is composed of integrated customs, traditions and current behaviour patterns of human group."
3. Brown is of the view that "Culture cannot be defined. It is better to describe it. The culture of a people is the way of life of that people, the things they value, their habits of life, their work of art, their music, their words, their history, briefly what they are, what they do and what they like."
4. Clyde Kluckhonn has observed, "Culture is a 'method of living' held by members of a particular society."
5. According to E.B. Tyler, "Culture is a complex which encompasses knowledge, faith, art, polity, law, customs and

other capacities and habits which an individual learns as a member of society."

6. Ellwood says, "Culture includes all of man's material civilisation, tools, weapons, clothing, shelter, machines and even system of industry."
7. Emerson observes, "The foundation of culture, as of character, is at last the moral sentiment."
8. Gandhiji remarks, "Culture is the foundation, the primary thing. It should show itself in the smallest detail of your conduct and personal behaviour, how you sit, how you walk, how you dress, etc. Inner culture must be reflected in your speech, the way in which you treat visitors and guests, and behave towards one another and towards your teachers and elders."
9. Nehru thinks, "Culture is the widening of the mind and of the spirit."
10. Rolph Linton defines culture in these words, "The culture of a society is a way of life of its members, the collection of ideas and habits which they learn, show and transmit from generation to generation."
11. Russell points out, "Genuine culture consists in being a citizen of the universe, not only of one or two arbitrary fragments of space and time. It helps man to understand human society as a whole, to estimate wisely the ends that communities pursue, and to see the present in its relation to past and future."
12. The University Education Commission 1948–49 writes, "Culture is an attitude of mind, an inclination of the spirit and those who yearn for it, wish to have a vision of greatness, sit in the presence of nobility, see the highest reach and scope of the spirit of man." According to the Commission, "Our art and literature, our law and history belong to the mainstream of our culture. Every Indian student should get to know the main outlines of the history of India, which is not a mere chronicle of date and defeats, of follies and failures. He should know the lives of the heroes who express the spirits of our civilisation, the seers of the Vedas, the Buddha and Sankara, Ashoka and Akbar. A habitual vision of greatness is the way to cultural growth."

A perusal of above definition would indicate that the views of the University Education Commission and Gandhiji truly reflect the true meaning of culture.

Dimensions of Culture: Classification – I

(1) Communal Culture
(2) Composite Culture
(3) Individual Culture
(4) National Culture
(5) Plural Culture
(6) World Culture

Dimensions of Culture: Classification – II

(1) *Material Culture* (Man made objects and things)
(2) *Non-material Culture* (Attitudes, Ideals, Values etc.)

Dimensions of Culture: Classification – III

(1) Narrow Dimension of Culture
(2) Broad Dimension of Culture

Chief Characteristics of Culture

1. Culture is acquired from one person to another
2. Culture is learnt from others
3. Culture is inherited
4. Culture is individual
5. Culture is social
6. Culture is fluid
7. Culture is manifested in the individual in several ways
8. Culture is static as well as dynamic
9. Culture is an integrating element of a society
10. Culture has various forms
11. Culture may differ from society to society
12. Some elements of culture are common
13. Culture is the diffusion as well as mingling of several races
14. Culture has wide connotations.

RELATIONSHIP BETWEEN CULTURE AND EDUCATION

Relationship between education and culture may be discussed under the under-mentioned ways:

1. Functions or the role of education towards culture
2. Functions or the role of culture towards education.

Education and culture are interrelated. Education as a part of culture has the twin functions of conservation and modification or renewal of the culture. Education is conceived as a systematic effort to maintain a culture. In its technical sense education is the process by which society, through schools, colleges, universities and other institutions, deliberately transmits its cultural heritage, its accumulated knowledge, values and skills from one generation to another.

Education is an instrument of cultural change. Education can impart knowledge, training and skill as well as inculcate new ideas and attitudes among the young.

It is the culture in which education germinates and flowers. It is the culture also upon which education exerts, in turn, a nourishing influence.

Role of Education Towards Culture

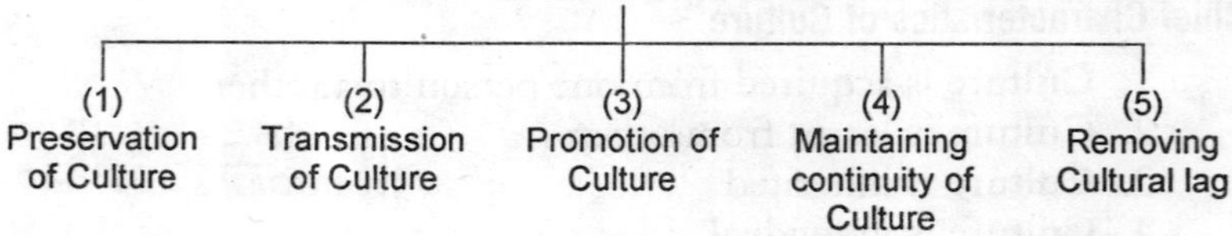

As a matter of fact all these functions of education towards culture are interlinked and they go side by side. Views of two thinkers are as under.

According to Percy Nunn, the special functions of education are:

1. To consolidate nation's spiritual strength,
2. To maintain nation's historic continuity,
3. To secure nation's past achievement,
4. To guarantee nation's future.

Ottaway is of the view that one of the tasks of education is to hand over the cultural values and behaviour patterns of the society to its young and potential members.

Influence of Culture on Education

Changing culture on account of scientific and technological advancement influences almost all areas of education i.e., aims of education, contents of education, teaching and learning methods and the role of the teacher.

CULTURAL HERITAGE OF INDIA AND VALUES

Cultural heritage implies the values of India held by it through the ages. These values and their sources are given below:

1. *The Vedic Vision.* It is imbued with a sense of toleration. It shows respect for the many paths to truth. It exhorts to be peaceful.
2. *Philosophy of Bhagwad Gita.* It states that action or duty is supreme and this is the basis of salvation. Duty well done without the expectation of reward leads to 'moksha.'
3. *Bhakti Marg.* It stresses two main points, i.e., love of God and love of man as the means of liberation.
4. *Central Concepts of Islam and Christianity.* Brotherhood of man and charity must be accepted as main principles of life.
5. *Muslim Sufis (mystic saints).* They also promoted love for God and love for man.
6. *Indian Nationalist Movement.* It was a very broad based movement in which people belonging to different creeds, faiths and religions etc., worked shoulder to shoulder for freedom. It emphasised national values.
7. *Influence of Sikhism.* Sikhism has exercised an important influence on Indian culture through the teachings of Guru Granth Sahib.
8. *Western Influence.* The western influence is also quite visible in our ways of life. It stresses rational values.

Role of Education in Resolving Conflicts, Ambivalence and Developing Tolerance

In Part VIII, the National Policy has emphasised 'value education' in the cultural perspective.

1. The growing concern over the erosion of essential values

and an increasing cynicism in society has brought to focus the need for readjustments in the curriculum in order to make education a forceful tool for the cultivation of social and moral values.

2. In our culturally plural society education should foster universal and eternal values, oriented towards the unity and integration of our people. Such value education should help eliminate obscurantism, religious fanaticism, violence, superstition and fatalism.
3. Apart from this combative role, value education has a profound positive content, based on our heritage, national goals and universal perceptions. It should lay primary emphasis on this aspect.

Summing up: Education is an instrument of cultural change. Education can impart knowledge, training and skill as well as inculcate new ideas, attitudes and values among the young.

RELIGIO-SPIRITUAL SOURCE OF VALUE

Religion and spirituality are inter related to a considerable extent. Both of them some common elements. Here we are primarily concerned with the ethical and moral values—enshrined in religion and spirituality. Religious rituals are not usually considered while discussing values.

MEANING AND DEFINITION OF RELIGION

Important definition of religion are:

Edward Tyler. "Religion refers to a faith in the spiritual power."

Emile Durkheim. "Religion is a unified set of beliefs and practices relative to sacred things, that is to say, things set apart and forbidden beliefs and practices which unite into one single moral community, called a Church to all those who adhere to them."

Malinowski. "Religion is a way of life, a system of beliefs and besides being a sociological event is a personal experience as well."

From the above definitions, it is observed that religion is a faith in the 'Supreme Power' or 'Divine' and is expressed through prayer and worship and other means of devotion.

Important Elements of Religion

Broadly speaking, every religion has the following elements:

1. *Personality of the Founder.* Charismatic and holy. (Excepting Hinduism, every religion has a founder)
2. *Genesis.* Subjects like creator and the universe created by Him, etc.
3. *Spiritualism.* Realisation of the self. Being one with Him. Liberation.
4. *Rituals.* Manners of worship, etc.
5. *Ethical and Moral Code.* Right or wrong etc.
6. *Sacred Places.* Places associated with the founder and religious leaders.
7. *Religious Literature.* Sacred books.
8. *Mythological Elements.*

All the above elements influence our values in varying degrees.

Religion does not consist in certain rites and rituals. It is a very narrow view of religion. "Unselfishness is the test of religion. He who has more of this unselfishness is nearer to Shiva. And if a man is selfish even though he has visited all the temples, seen all the places of pilgrimage, and painted himself like a leopard, he is still farther off from Shiva," writes Swami Vivekananda. At some other place he writes, "I do not care for liberation, I would rather go to a hundred thousand hells doing good to others (silently) like the spring, this is my religion." True religion is the motive power behind all ethical and moral codes. No boy or girl can be counted as properly educated unless he or she knows the religious interpretation of life.

About moral values and religion, Gandhiji writes, "For me morals, ethics and religion are convertible terms. A moral life without religion is like a house built on sand."

According to Dr. Radhakrishnan, "True religion is in the heart of man, not in the man-made creeds. If you become merely a '*Sakasra*'—literate man— and you do not have the moral principles and you do not cultivate wisdom, what will happen to you? You will become a '*Raksasa*'—an evil person."

Ross's view is, "It is through religion that the youth can be set on the road to the pursuits of the absolute values: truth, goodness and beauty."

VALUE-ORIENTED EDUCATION THOUGHTS FROM RELIGIOUS SCRIPTURES

Value-Oriented Thoughts from Hindu Scriptures

Yajurveda

- Do good to humanity.
- Enjoy your own wealth and covet not the wealth of others.
- Earn wealth in a righteous way.
- Shun crookedness.
- Live in a spirit of friendliness with all.
- Noble qualities give peace of mind, widespread fame; add to one's greatness. Practice of truth give ease and concentration of mind gives strength.
- Perform noble deeds, develop intellect and purify your mind.

Manu

- Cultivate the firmness of mind and contentment.
- Cultivate the spirit of forgiveness under all circumstances.
- Devote your mind to virtues and observe abstinence from the entertainment of sinful thoughts.
- Do not be dishonest by taking a thing without the permission of its owner though fraud, hypocrisy or breach of faith or by teaching falsely.
- Keep mental purity by freeing yourself from inordinate love or hatred, from prejudice or injustice etc.
- Fellow path of rectitude and freedom from sin.
- Develop your intellect by seeking the company of the noble and learned.
- Harmonise your thoughts, words and deeds.
- Cultivate peace of mind and calmness.

Ram Charitmanas

- There is no virtue like benevolence, and no meanness like oppressing others.
- There is no other kinship except that of devotion.

Value-Thoughts from Other Religions

Christianity

- You shall honour your father and mother.
- You shall not kill.

- You shall not commit adultery.
- You shall not steal.
- You shall not bear false witness against your neighbour.
- You shall not covet your neighbour's wife.
- You shall not covet your neighbour's goods.

Islam

- Be honest in exchange of things.
- Do not acquire another's substance wrongfully.
- Do not sell inferior and low-quality things.
- Do not bribe.
- Do not be unjust to others.

Sikhism

- Truth is higher, but higher still is truthful living.
- There can be no worship without good action.
- God's eye of mercy falls on those who take care of lowest.
- The life of speaking God's grace is not to be of idle mysticism but of active service done in the midst of worldly relations.

Buddhism

- Have right understanding.
- Have right thought.
- Have right speech.
- Do right action.
- Earn right livelihood.
- Do right effort.
- Have right mindfulness.
- Cultivate right concentration.

Jainism

- Have right faith.
- Have right knowledge.
- Have right conduct.

A FEW EXAMPLES OF HUMAN VALUES AS CONTAINED IN VARIOUS RELIGIONS

Control of Anger

Buddhism: One should not give way to anger, but control it.
Christianity: The mark of a Christian is love, not hatred.

Confucianism: One should so conduct oneself so as to avoid hatred or anger for others.

Hinduism: Anger breeds confusion.

Islam: The strong man is only he who controls himself when he is angry.

Jainism: Anger is not for the wise or the religious.

Judaism: Anger causes strife and destruction.

Sikhism: Anger is the fire that burns us as at cremation.

Taoism: Return anger with goodness.

Zoroastrianism: Never give way to the deadly emotion of anger.

Brotherhood

Buddhism: One should make good men one's closest friends.

Confucianism: Friendship and brotherhood are the cardinal virtues.

Hinduism: The good man makes no distinction between friend and foe, brother and stranger but regards them all with impartiality.

Islam: All men are brothers and should live as such.

Jainism: Treat all men as brothers at all times.

Judaism: God has made all men brothers and they should live together as brothers at all times.

Sikhism: Get together, my brethren. And remove all misunderstanding through regard for each other.

Duty

Buddhism: One should be faithful to one's duty at all times.

Christianity: One has a duty to God and duties towards one's fellows.

Confucianism: The wise man makes duty his aim at all times.

Hinduism: Never falter in doing your duty.

Islam: All men who do their duty will receive a fitting reward from Lord.

Jainism: It is the duty of all to be impartial.

Sincerity

Buddhism: God loves the earnest, sincere man.

Christianity: At all times the true Christian is sincere.

Confucianism: Heaven will help the man who is sincere.

Hinduism: The Lord does not favour those who are not sincere and honest.

Islam: God knows whether or not a man is earnest in his

professions and will deal with all men accordingly.

Jainism: The Lord will help those who are earnest.

Sikhism: Earnestness is the only basis for true religious acts.

Work

Buddhism: Work, and not birth, determines one's place in the world.

Christianity: A man is to be judged by his works.

Confucianism: Not ease, but work in the mark of a good man.

Hinduism: The man who does good becomes good.

"*National Curriculum Framework*" (2000) has recommended education about religion and not religious values. Awareness of religions has been conceived as one of the major source of values. The Framework observed, "What is required today is not religious education but education about religion, their basics, the values inherent therein and also a comparative study of the philosophy of all religions. These need to be inculcated at appropriate stages of education right from primary years. Students have to be given awareness that the essence of every religion is common, only the practices differ." The students should also be led to believe that differences of opinion in certain areas are also to be respected (p. 19). The Framework has added an element of caution:

"Education about religion must be handled with great care. All steps must be taken in advance to ensure that no personal prejudice or narrow minded perception are allowed to distort the real purpose of this venture and no rituals, dogmas and superstitions are propagated in the name of education about religion. All religions therefore are to be treated with equal respect (*Sarva Dharma Sambhav*) and there has to be no discrimination on the ground of any religion (*Pathanirapekstata*) (p. 20).

VALUES AS SHRINED IN THE INDIAN CONSTITUTION

The values cherished by the Indian people today are enshrined in the Constitution of India. These permeate the Constitution as a whole. However, following are the most important parts of the Constitution in this regard.

One. The Preamble of the Constitution

Two. Part III dealing with Fundamental Rights

Tł ee. Part IV containing Directive Principles of State Policy.

Prean ıble

The Preamble is the most precious part of the Constitution. It is considered as the soul of the Constitution. It is the key to the Constitution.

The Preamble is reproduced below:

WE, THE PEOPLE OF INDIA, having solemnly resolved to constitute India into a SOVEREIGN SOCIALIST SECULAR DEMOCRATIC REPUBLIC and to secure to all its citizens:

JUSTICE, social, economic and political;

LIBERTY of thought, expression, belief, faith and worship;

EQUALITY of status and opportunity, and to promote among them all;

FRATERNITY assuring the dignity of the individual and the unity and integrity of the Nation:

IN OUR CONSTITUENT ASSEMBLY this twenty-sixth day of November, 1949, do HEREBY ADOPT, ENACT AND GIVE TO OURSELVES THIS CONSTITUTION.

Note: The words 'SOCIALIST,' 'SECULAR' and 'integrity' were added by the Constitution (Forty-Second Amendment) Act, 1976.

VALUES OF SOCIALISM AS ENSHRINED IN THE INDIAN CONSTITUTION

Gandhiji saw socialism as a way of life. He called it 'Sarvodaya Samaj' in which the 'greatest good of all' is the end. He explained his concept of socialism in an article in 1947 under the captain 'Who is a Socialist?' He wrote, "Under Socialism all the members of society are equal—none low, none high. Under it the prince and the peasant, the wealthy and the poor, the employer and the employee are all on the same level." He further observed, "Socialism requires crystal—like (pure) means to achieve it. Only truthful, non-violent and pure-hearted socialists will be able to establish a socialist society in India and the world."

The distinguishing values of socialism are:

1. Equality between man and man.
2. Humane outlook to be the basis of economic system.

3. Due respect to the personality of the individual and no disregard to it for the sake of material gains.
4. Stress on equality, freedom and social justice.
5. Free expression of views.
6. Non-violent means to achieve ends.
7. Sharing natural resources and power.
8. Social welfare services.

VALUES OF SOCIAL AND ECONOMIC EQUALITY

Significance of Value of Equality. The French Revolution and the American Declaration of Independence, among other values, were based on the concept of equality.

Equality is one of the important pillars of Democracy.

Equality implies:

1. All persons are provided with adequate opportunities for the development of their personalities.
2. No class or caste is given special privileges which are denied to others.
3. Rights are equally distributed among all.
4. All have equal access to opportunities leading to equality.

Every citizen is expected to understand the meaning of equality and to strive for the realisation of the objective of this value. One of the primary functions of the state is to ensure that the underlying elements of this values are fully taken note of in its all endeavours.

Equality in the Constitution of India

Following are the various provisions:

1. *Preamble*. It mentions 'Equality of status and opportunity.'
2. *Fundamental Rights*. *Article 14*. Equality before law. *Article 15*. Prohibition of discrimination on grounds of religion, race, caste, sex or place of birth. *Article 16*. Equality of opportunity in public employment.
3. *Article 17*. Abolition of untouchability.
4. *Article 32*. Right to constitutional remedies.

Types of Equality

Natural	*Political*	*Social*	*Economic*	*Legal*	*Religious*
Every individual is equal as human being.	1. Free and fair elections.	1. Equality of both sexes	1. No concentration of wealth in a few hands.	1. Rule of law.	Equal opportunity to profess one's faith
	2. Universal adult franchise.	2. No discrimination on any ground.	2. Equitable distribution of national resources	2. Same law applicable to everyone	
	3. Equal right to contest elections and hold				

Social and Economic Equality for Human Development

Dr. B.R. Ambedkar, the chairman of the drafting committee of the Constitution of India; in his final address to the Constituent Assembly on November 25, 1949, very rightly stressed the importance of social and economic equality in these words:

"On the social plane, we have in India a society based on the principles of graded inequality which means elevation of some and degradation of other, on the economic plane we have a society in which there are some who have immense wealth as against many who live in abject poverty. On the 26th January, 1950, we are going to enter into a life of contradictions. In politics we will have equality and in social and economic life, we will have inequality. In politics, we will be recognising the principle of one man one vote and one vote one value. In our social and economic life, we shall by reason of our social and economic structure, continue to deny the principle of one man one value. How long shall we continue to live this life of contradiction? How long shall we continue to deny equality in our social and economic life? If we continue to deny it for long, we will do so by putting our political democracy in peril. We must remove this contradiction at the earliest possible moment or else those who suffer from inequality will blow up the structure of political democracy."

Values of Equality and their Educational Implications

There are three important elements of the value of equality which must be fully addressed to:

One. All students in the educational institutions should be treated by the teachers on equal basis i.e., same treatment should be given to the children belonging to deprived sections as to others.

Two. The significance of acquiring the value of equality and its practice should be emphasised.

Three. Facilities for pursuing education should be provided on a large scale to the deprived sections of the society.

On the aspect of equality the Indian Education Commission (1964–66) has observed, "One of the important social objectives of education is to equalise opportunities enabling the backward or underprivileged classes and individuals to use education as a lever for the improvement of their condition. Every society that values social justice and is anxious to improve the lot of the common man and cultivate all available talent, must ensure progressive equality of opportunity to all sections of the population. This is the only guarantee for the building up of an egalitarian human society in which the exploitation of the weak will be minimised."

Equal Opportunity does not Mean Identical Education. There is no doubt that no two individuals are alike. They differ in tastes, manner, attitudes and aptitudes, beliefs etc. Any attempt to provide precisely the same educational programmes and opportunities is likely to be met with failure. Equal opportunity implies that the rich and the poor alike should have equal access to the educational system and programmes without any hindrance. All material barriers should be removed. Caste, colour or creed should not put any check on an individual to pursue course of education in accordance with his ability and aptitude.

How does Inequality of Educational Opportunities arise? The Education Commission listed the following causes:

1. Lack of educational facilities.
2. Poverty of a large section of population and indifference to education.
3. Differences in standards of educational institutions.
4. Differences in home environments.
5. Disparity in outlook of the people regarding education of boys and girls.

6. Disparity due to advanced classes and backward classes.
7. High private cost of education.

The National Policy on Education, 1986 as modified in 1992 has also laid great stress on the removal of disparities and to equalise educational opportunity by attending to the specific needs of the following groups:

1. Education for women's equality.
2. Education of the Scheduled Castes.
3. Education of the Scheduled Tribes.
4. Other Educationally Backward Sections and Areas.
5. Minorities.
6. The Handicapped.

Ways and Means of Providing Maximum Equality and Reducing Inequality of Opportunity in Education

1. Tuition free education to weaker sections of society.
2. Free textbooks and uniform to weaker sections of society.
3. Establishment of book banks.
4. Grant for the purchase of books to the needy students.
5. Adequate number of scholarships to talented students.
6. Loans on nominal rates of interest.
7. Transport facilities according to means.
8. 'Earning and Learning' facilities.
9. Establishment of hostels for the weaker sections and charging nominal rates.

CONSTITUTION AS SOURCE OF SECULAR VALUES

Meaning of Secular Values

Secular values derive their meaning from the word 'Secularism.'

The Indian concept of secularism is expressed in the following often quoted principles:

(i) *Sarva-dharma-samantva* or *Sarva-dharma-sambhava*—equal regard for all faiths and creeds.
(ii) *Ekam Brahma Vipra Bahuda Vadanti*—God is one, wise men call Him by different names.

Although the word secularism was introduced only in 1976 in our Constitution, our secularism is historical. We have had great breadth of vision as expressed above.

Ashoka's secular outlook is one of the landmarks not only of Indian civilisation but also of the human civilisation. He made a passionate appeal for developing a spirit of reverence and tolerance for all faiths.

Dr. B.R. Ambedkar, the principal architect of our Constitution explains the concept of a Secular Sate in these words, "Secular State does not mean that it shall not take into consideration the religious sentiments of the people. All that Secular State means is that the Parliament shall not be competent to impose any particular religion upon the rest of the people."

Dr. Rajendra Prasad, the first President of India has very clearly explained the concept of secularism in the Indian context, "There are some who think that because we are a Secular State, we do not believe in religion or spiritual values. Far from being so, it really means that in this country all are free to profess or preach the faith of their liking and that we wish well of all religions and want than to develop in their own way without any hindrance."

Secular Values or Secular Outlook or Characteristics of a Secular-Minded Individual

Following salient features of secularism emerge from the above stated views:

1. Secular values treat all religions on an equal footing.
2. Secular values accept freedom of religion.
3. Secular values imply freedom of worship.
4. Secular values imply tolerance.
5. Secular values encourage rational thinking.
6. Secular values view all citizens with equal rights.
7. Secular values encourage moral and spiritual values.
8. Secular values believe in co-existence.
9. Secular values stress free inquiry.
10. Secular values mean freedom of mind from dogmatic ideas.
11. Secular outlook is not a negation of religion.

Constitutional Provisions on Secularism

Often a question has been raised if India, it being a Secular State is not in essence hostile towards religion? The answer is an emphatic 'No.' This becomes very clear from the following provisions of the Constitution of India.

1. *Article 15. Prohibition of Discrimination on Grounds of Religion, Race, Caste, Sex or Place of Birth.* (i) The State shall not discriminate against any citizen on grounds only of religion, race, caste, sex, place of birth or any of them. (ii) No citizen on grounds only of religion, race, sex, place of birth shall be denied access to shops, wells, tanks, etc.
2. *Article 25(1). Freedom of Conscience.* According to this Article, all citizens are equally entitled to freedom of conscience and the right to profess, practise and propagate religion. However, while the freedom of conscience is absolute i.e., without any restriction, the exercise of freedom of propagation of religion is subject to restrictions in the interest of harmony, public morality and order.
3. *Article 27. Exemption from the Payment of Taxes.* As per this Article, no person shall be compelled to pay any taxes, the proceeds of which are specifically appropriated in payment of expenses for the promotion or maintenance of any particular religion or religious denomination.

Salient Characteristics of Indian Secular State

1. Indian State treats all religions on equal footing.
2. Indian State neither interferes with nor promotes any religion.
3. It permits individual and collective freedom of religion to all citizens.
4. It views all individuals as citizens with equal rights and not as members of any particular religious group.
5. It is not against any religion.
6. It functions in a way independent of religion.
7. It allows religious education in some educational institutions run and managed by minorities subject to certain conditions.

Educational Implications: Reasons for Imparting Secular Values

1. Secular values develop a moral outlook.
2. Secular values help in the development of liberal attitudes and values.

3. Secular values develop wider-vision.
4. Secular values develop an attitude of appreciation and understanding of others' point of view.
5. Secular values develop democratic values.
6. Secular values develop scientific temper of mind.
7. Secular values develop humanistic outlook.
8. Secular values synthesise materialism and spiritualism.
9. Secular values serve as an antidote to religious fanaticism and hatred.

Summing up: Secular values accord an important places to ethical, moral and spiritual values. These must be inculcated in the students through value education.

CONSTITUTION AS SOURCE OF DEMOCRATIC VALUES

Meaning of Democracy

With a view to understand democratic values, we may first of all go through the meaning of democracy for democratic values emerge from it.

Meaning of Democracy in Political Context: The word democracy is derived from the Greek word '*Demos*' meaning 'people' and '*karatos*' meaning 'powers.' Democracy thus means power of the people.

Cleon, a Greek philosopher defined democracy in 422 B.C. in these words, "That shall be democratic which shall be of the people, by the people, for the people."

Like Cleon, US President Abraham Lincoln (1809–1865 A.D.) defined it as "Democracy is the government of the people, for the people and by the people."

According to Lord Bryce, "The word democracy has been used ever since the time of Herodotus (5th century B.C.) to denote that form of government in which the ruling power of a state is legally vested, not in any particular class or classes but in the members of the community as a whole."

Sir John Seelay defines democracy as "Government in which everyone has a share."

Democracy as a Way of Life. A very appropriate definition of democracy is found in the observations of the University Education Commission. According to the Commission, "Democracy is the way of life and not a mere political arrangement. It is based on the principles of equal freedom and equal right for its members regardless of race, religion, sex, occupation or economic stature." Thus 'equal freedom' and 'equal right' are the watchwords of democracy.

U.S. President F.D. Roosevelt (1882–1945) states "Democracy is not a mere matter of universal suffrage and unhampered expression of the popular will. It must be a positive and constructive force in the daily life of the people and provide not merely for political but economic ends also."

C.C. Maxey in 'Political Philosophies' has given a very comprehensive view of democracy, "Democracy as re-interpreted in the twentieth century is thus seen to be more than a political formula, more than a system of government, more than a social order. It is a search for a way of life—the best way for all mankind, the way most in keeping with the nature of man and the nature of the universe."

Significance of Each Letter of the Work Democracy: Values Cherished by Citizens or Democratic Values

The spirit of democracy as a way of life and a form of government may be explained by assigning ideals and values to each letter of democracy.

'D' stands for —Division of authority and power or sharing.
—Dignity and worth of the individual.
—Duty-Consciousness.

'E' stands for —Endurance.
—Equality.
—Ethical values.

'M' stands for—Mental alertness.
—Mutual understanding.
—Mass education.

'O' stands for —Objective attitude.
—Open mindedness

'C' stands for —Classless society.
—Cooperation.
—Courage, courtesy.

'R' stands for —Rational thinking.
—Respect for others' ideas
—Right relationship between rights and responsibilities.

'A' stands for —Anti-touchability.

—'Appreciation of others' culture and belief.
—Adult franchise.
—Adult education.

'C' stands for —Caring and concern for others.
—Compassion
—Constructive and creative attitude.

'Y' stands for —Yearning for living and working together harmoniously.
—Yearning for peace.

In short, value education in democracy is needed on account of the following reasons:

1. To enable the individual to acquire the knowledge of rights and duties.
2. To develop in the citizens humane qualities.
3. To develop in the citizens faith in the peaceful methods of solving issues.
4. To enable the citizens to fulfil their constitutional obligations.
5. To enable the citizens to develop a rational outlook.
6. To enable the citizens to reflect upon pros and cons of the election manifestos of political parties.

Methods for Developing Democratic Values

1. Personal examples of the staff.
2. Associating students with the running of some programmes of the schools.
3. Organising student self-government in schools.
4. Emphasising self-discipline.
5. Giving due consideration to student's personality.

6

Methods of Teaching Human Values: Direct, Indirect, Integrating Values with Curricular and Co-curricular Activities

METHODS OF TEACHING HUMAN VALUE AS SUGGESTED BY KOTHARI COMMISSION OR EDUCATION COMMISSION (1964–1966)

The Commission observed that the teaching of values should be done both by direct and indirect manner, by suggestion as well as discussion in teaching. It stated, "We attach great importance to the role of indirect influence in building up good character. The school atmosphere, the personality and behaviour of the teachers and the facilities provided in the school will have a large say in developing a sense of values. We would like to emphasise that the consciousness of values must permeate the whole curriculum and the programme of activities in the school. It is not only the teachers in charge of moral instruction who are responsible for building character. Every teacher, whatever be the subject, must necessarily accept this responsibility. He must ensure that in the teaching of his particular subject and in his dealings with pupils, fundamental values such as integrity and social responsibility are brought out. The teacher need not, we can even say that he should not, try to draw out the underlying moral all the time; but if he has given some thought to the values underlying the scope of his subject and his work as a teacher, they will imperceptibly pass into his teaching and make an impact on the minds of his students. Moreover, a sense of purpose should inspire all school activities and must be reflected in the life, tone and atmosphere of the school. The school assembly, the curricular and co-curricular activities, the celebration of religious festivals of all religions, work experience, team games and sports, subject clubs, social service programmes—all these can help in inculcating the values of cooperation and mutual regard, honesty and integrity, discipline and social responsibility. These values have a special significance in Indian society today when young men and women are passing through a crisis of character. (Para 8, 95, pp. 358-59).

In addition to this indirect approach for inculcating moral and spiritual values, we consider that specific provision for direct moral instruction in the school programmes is highly desirable. We agree with the recommendation of the Sri Prakasa Committee that one or two periods a week should be set aside in the school time-table for instruction in moral and spiritual values. At the primary stage such instruction will generally be imparted through interesting stories, including stories drawn from the great religions of the world. At the secondary stage, there may be frequent discussions between the teachers and the pupils on the values sought to be inculcated. Whatever be the method of teaching it should not lead to moral instruction being divorced from the rest of the curriculum or being confined to a single period. If the values are to become a part of the student's character, an all-embracing treatment of the moral way of life is needed." (Para 8, 96, p. 359).

VALUES ARE CAUGHT AS WELL AS TAUGHT

At the outset it must be stated that values can be taught as well as caught. With a view to learn to painting, one has to learn the rules of painting and practise the art of painting. Likewise for learning how to swim, one has to learn the rules and then to plunge and swim. Similar is the case of learning music. In the case of human value development also, value clarification and practice are needed. A synthesis of these two elements would result in the suggestion that in the process of education for value development, methods appropriate to volition and affection should be more proponent. Nevertheless, appropriate methods to cognition also have a significant role to play.

BROAD CLASSIFICATION OF METHODS OF TEACHING HUMAN VALUES

Broad Classification of Methods of Teaching Human Values

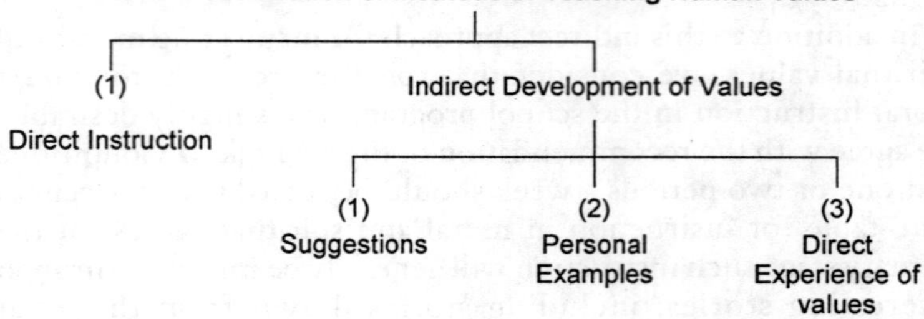

It may be stressed that we should not depend on one particular method. All should be used in an integrative way. However, it is generally accepted that indirect methods are more effective in developing values.

METHODS OF TEACHING HUMAN VALUES/INSTRUCTIONAL METHODOLOGIES

Methods

1. Story telling
2. Discussion/panel discussion, symposia, seminar, round table, etc.
   - 2.1 discussion based on pictures
   - 2.2 discussion based on life situation
   - 2.3 discussion based on newspaper
   - 2.4 discussion based on contents of letters
   - 2.5 discussion based on songs
   - 2.6 discussion based on films and filmstrips
   - 2.7 discussion based on religious books.
3. Self-study by students
4. Visits to places of religious social and spiritual importance
   - 4.1 visits to places of worship of different religions and associated with saints and seers.
   - 4.2 visits to hospitals/asylums
   - 4.3 visits to creches
   - 4.4 visits to offices, municipal board/district board

4.5 visits to institutions for special education of the handicapped

4.6 visits to factories/farms in the neighbourhood.

5. Participation in prayer services
6. Dramatisation/role-playing
7. Talks by eminent speakers
8. Brains trust
9. Debates
10. Games
11. Creative writing
12. Preparation of scrap books
13. Preparation of drawing sketches
14. Workshop
15. Project work
16. Celebration of festivals
17. Question-box
18. Laboratory method
19. Brainstorming
20. Team learning
21. Programmed learning.

Appropriate Methodologies for Different Age groups/Classes

Age Group	*Classes*	*Appropriate Methodologies*
(6+)—(7+)	I and II	1: 2.1: 2.5: 2.6: 6:10.
(8+)—(10+)	III, IV & V	1: 2.1: 2.5: 2.6: 6: 10: 4: 12: 13: 16.
(11+)—(13+)	VI, VII, VIII	2.1: 2.2: 2.3: 2.6: 2.7: 4: 5: 6: 9: 10: 12: 13: 15: 16: 20: 21: 22.
(14+)—(15+)	IX, X	2.1: 2.2: 2.3: 2.4 2.5: 2.7: 3: 4: 5: 6: 7: 8: 9: 10: 14: 15: 16: 17: 19: 20: 21.
(16+)—(17+)	XI & XII	2.3: 2.4: 2.7: 3: 7: 8: 11: 14: 15: 17: 18: 19: 20: 21.

INTEGRATING VALUES WITH CO-CURRICULAR PROGRAMME

Value education programme should form an integral element of co-curricular programme of the school. In this context, the following programme should receive due attention.

Instructional Material	*Methods*
1. Group devotional songs—with simple musical instruments	1. Guiding group singing
2. Patriotic songs and folk songs	2. Choral singing
3. Sarva Dharma prayers	3. (a) Group/community singing (b) Silent seating/meditation
4. Sayings and quotations	4. Collection, display, reading, recitation, memorisation, group discussion
5. Short plays and dialogues	5. Reading, recitation, dramatisation, role-play followed by discussion
6. Themes for mime	6. Miming followed by discussion
7. Incidents, events, episodes from life situations for role-play	7. Role-play and discussion
8. Poems and passages for recitation	8. Collection, display, recitation, reading, writing memorisation, discussion, assignment in forms of question-answer
9. Passages and episodes from biographies and autobiographies	9. Collection, reading, writing, discussion and summarisation
10. Stories-fables, parables, myths, folk tales, fairy tales, animal tales, etc.	10. Collection, reading, dramatisation, picturisation and making kits like masks, costumes, etc.
11. Descriptions of places—cultural, historical, religious, scientific, industrial and of national importance including zoos, museums, etc.	11. Collection of materials and pictures, reading of materials, discussion, observations and recording and writing reports
12. Selection from literature—novels, essays, etc.	12. Selection, reading, writing, summarising, passages, picking up significant statements and incidents etc.
13. Descriptions of life styles of various lands and faiths	13. Collection, reading, discussion, presenting the significant details, interviewing, experiencing living in families with people of different life styles
14. Periodicals for pupils and teachers	14. Selection of appropriate material from periodicals for discussion and presentation, paper clipping, scrap books, etc.
15. (a) Slides, (b) film strips, (c) films, (d) tapes, (e) records	15. Preparation, demonstration and feed-back discussion
16. Charts, pictures, posters and models	16. Preparation, display, use and discussion
17. Material such as write-ups, pictures, models of festivals (a) national (b) religious	17. Selection, reading, discussion, assignment, participation and celebrations (including exhibitions)

Instructional Material	Methods
18. Quiz and games to give learning experience	18. Organising and conducting
19. Equipment and material for activities such as (i) cultural (ii) recreational (iii) social service (iv) creative, etc.	19. Preparation and use
20. Puppets and dolls	20. Preparation and use
21. First-aid kit	21. Learning, participating and using appropriately
22. Museums	22. Collections, development and use

Notes: (i) Hardware material related to above may be added up.

(ii) These materials can be presented in the form of:

(a) Text-books

(b) Work books

(c) Hand books for teachers

(d) Reference books for teachers

(e) General reading material for children

(f) Teaching-learning side to be used or categorised as found appropriate

List of Activities

1. Assembly
2. Music period, painting period, dance period, clay work period
3. News and thought
4. Dramatic club
5. Recitation, declamation, debate, clubs
6. Story-telling and writing, essay writing, quiz, general knowledge, competitions
7. Class magazine and school magazine
8. Excursions and visits
9. Library and audio-visual periods
10. Exhibitions class-wise and school
11. Wall magazine and class display boards
12. Functions and celebrations
13. Production-oriented programme
14. Community service programme
15. SUPW Programme—music, vocal, instrumental, dance, theatre, craft, clay modelling and ceramics, painting, batik, commercial arts, carpentry, photography, electrical gadgets

and repairs, knitting, and needle work, preservation of food, etc.

16. Zero period
17. Open-ended period
18. Cultural programme—housewise
19. Monitor system
20. Prefactorial system
21. Games and sports
22. House system
23. NCC
24. *Yoga*
25. Road safty care
26. Scouts and guides
27. Residential camps and retreats
28. Students' days (self-teaching days)
29. Special education centre
30. Residential teaching—cooperative learning
31. First aid club
32. Blind Relief
33. Hospital service
34. Blood donation camp
35. Leadership development programme
36. Counselling service
37. Preparation of exhibits
38. Guest speakers
39. PTA (parent meet)
40. Old students' association
41. Workshops and seminar
42. Staff development programme
43. Staff-club
44. Staff-meeting
45. Creative expressions
46. Self-accounting
47. Tree planting
48. Waste material bank for improvisation
49. Autobiographies by children
50. Daily diary
51. Question-Box
52. Personal hygiene
53. Self-help for cleaning

54. Helping parents at home
55. Preparing letters to the authorities relating the civic problems
56. Savings in cash and kind for helping the community.

Notes:(i) It is intended that the schools will choose appropriate material and activities and adopt methods in organising them depending upon the situations existing in the school with reference to physical and material resources.

(ii) The lists are only illustrative of any good school programme with reference to moral education now under consideration. Special attention will have to paid by the institutions in focussing the whole programme towards the attainment of specific values.

(iii) It may be noted that the achievement of the objectives will only be possible by a cooperative planning and execution by both teachers and students. It is necessary to orient the entire staff in this regard.

(iv) It is obvious that some of the activities are classroom activities, some daily routine activities of the entire school, some arranged on the specific occasion on some days and a few to be built up over a long period of time.

(v) Irrespective of whether only a few activities or a large number of them are undertaken, self-evaluation procedures by the staff and children in various forms like, accounting, keeping diaries, writing reports, autobiographies, etc., may be adopted in relation to value development.

(vi) It may be noted that some of the activities and programmes need involvement of the school, parent and community together.

(vii) It may be realised that the success of the above programme depends upon cooperative endeavour and involvement of school, home and community.

TEACHING HUMAN VALUES: MODULE I. PROGRAMME SUGGESTED BY THE NATIONAL SEMINAR HELD AT COIMBATORE BY RAMAKRISHNA MISSION VIDYALAYA, FEBRUARY, 1980

I. Pre-school Stage (Nursery School, Balwadi or Pre-primary School

Major Objective

The major objective at the pre-school stage is to give such education to the young child as to inculcate in him all the desirable values and help him develop into a wholesome personality. Since there is no need for a set syllabus at the pre-school level, the ethical and social values can be inculcated through the daily activities of the pre-school.

The Major Activities in a Pre-school are Generally:

1. Prayer
2. Informal talks
3. Outdoor free play
4. Indoor free play
5. Music
6. Story-telling
7. Creative experience
8. Science experiences
9. Dramatisation
10. Field trips
11. Celebrations of festivals and national days.

Ethical and Social Values can be Inculcated Through Activities by Helping Children to:

1. Share play materials.
2. Wait for their turn to get the materials.
3. Care for play and other materials.
4. Replace the material safely after use.
5. Play with other children of different age ranges and help the children who are in difficulty.
6. Learn the rules and regulations of various games and abide by them.
7. Engage in cooperative play.
8. Listen to informal talks by the teacher and talk to the teacher about values.
9. Observe cleanliness while washing their hands before and after eating food, while going to the toilet and while washing their plates.
10. Understand the significance of celebrating various festivals and national days.
11. Participate in the celebrations.
12. Develop a sense of patriotism.
13. Listen to classical stories such as those from *Ramayana*, *Mahabharata*, *Bible*, *Quran*, *etc.* and others and understand the morals illustrated by them.

14. Sing songs which will inculcate moral and ethical values.
15. Keep pets in the school, help develop the values of love, affection, kindness and sympathy.
16. Learn values through dramatisation of:
    (a) Christmas
    (b) Pongal
    (c) Deepavali
    (d) Krishna Jayanti
    (e) Saraswati pooja
    (f) Sri Guru Maharaj (Ramakrishna Paramhansa) Jayanti
    (g) Holi Mother Sri Sarda Devi's birth day
    (h) Buddha
    (i) Swami Vivekananda
    (j) Mahatma Gandhi
    (k) Vinayaka Chaturthi
    (l) Shivaji
    (m) Jawaharlal Nehru
    (n) Farmer, cobbler, shopman, doctor, policeman, postman and others
    (o) Episodes from the lives of other great men and women like Rani of Jhansi, Sarojini Naidu, Avvaiyar Kannaki, Joan of Arc and others
17. See suitable films
18. Receive appreciation when they do something good; and
19. They are accepted and recognised in all their activities

Note: Specific local environment and needs may also be taken note of while organising such programmes.

Types of Guide-books Needed

1. Stories
2. Songs
3. Games
4. Pictures, puzzles, posters, charts and other audio-visual aids.

Orientation to Teachers

Orientation must be given for a minimum of two weeks in Home Science Colleges teachers training institutions, which are involved in pre-school/*balwadi* training and administration.

Links

Link must be established with the primary schools through attaching pre-primary section to them.

II. Primary School Stage (Classes 1 to 5)

The outline of the syllabus for the primary stage is in three parts:

Part I gives a list of activities which must be followed in all the primary schools in appropriate ways to develop the essential ethical and social values. These activities are common to all the five classes. Part II gives suggestions for integrating ethical and social values with the existing school subjects and Part III offers some suggestions for certain co-curricular activities, all or some of which, may be carried out according to the facilities and experience available in primary schools.

Part I. Activities Common to All Pupils

Activity	*Values to be developed*
1. Morning assembly	Punctuality, faith in God, team spirit and orderliness
2. Flag hoisting	Patriotism and discipline
3. Campus cleaning	Cleanliness, cooperation, dignity of labour
4. Bhajans and group-singing	Team spirit, faith in God, appreciation for finer expressions
5. Cultural programme	Cooperation, following rules, good manners and sense of responsibility
6. Group games and sports	Cooperation, consideration for others, sense of responsibility. Following rules and regulations and sportsmanship
7. Celebration of national days	National spirit, cooperation, national integration
8. Celebration of religious festivals	Faith in God, consideration for others, respecting worship and worthy rituals
9. Assisting in the mid-day meals in the school	Cooperation, caring for public property, service-mindedness, dependability and sympathy

Part II: Integrating Ethical and Social Values with School Subjects

School subject for integration	Ways of integration
1. Language	Include in the text and supplementary readers stories, essays and songs suitable for the development of values.
2. Science	Include specific lessons aimed at developing values of cleanliness, personal hygiene, habits of environmental hygiene, honesty and scientific attitude.
3. History	Narrate lives of great leaders of the world and the values for which they stood and taught.
4. Current events	Highlight the heroic, national or international events, taken from the daily newspapers, to develop values such as consideration for others, national spirit, civic sense, cooperation and pride in the community.
5. Moral instruction	Carry out the items given in the present syllabus prescribed by the State in the moral lesson classes and also integrate them with others lessons.

The following themes will be useful to teachers and students:

Class	Stories (in English)	Values
1.	The Tamil Poetess Avvaiyar and Lord Murugan, Jesus and children, Emperor Pari and his help to a jasmine plant, Four cows and the lion, The lion and the mouse.	Develop orderly movements, fearlessness, cooperation, good manners, unselfishness and desire to serve.
2.	(Ramayana), Gandhiji and truth, Lord Krishna's message to Arjuna, Dhuruvan, Prahalad, Sri Rama Krishna Paramhansa, Swami Vivekananda.	Respect for elders, truthfulness, faith in God, valour and courage.
3.	Buddha, Jesus, Asoka, Appar, Sundarar, Tulsi Das, Manickavasagar, Jawaharlal Nehru, Holy Mother Sarda Devi.	National spirit, truthfulness, love for others and integrity, hospitality and purity in life.
4.	National leaders Motilal Nehru, Thiruppur Kumaran, Netaji Subhas Chandra Bose, Ishwar Chandra Vidyasagar, Rabindranath Tagore, international leaders: Helen Keller, Abraham Lincoln, Booker Washington, Thoreau, John Ruskin, etc.	National spirit, understanding culture and similar texts and poets, saints and great men available in each cultural and language region of the country and culture of other nations, perseverance, respect for hard work.
5.	Confucius, Zorashtra, Albert Switzer, B.R. Ambedkar etc	Leadership qualities, social justice, sharing and serving the poor.

Similar topics could be used for songs and children taught soul-lifting melody.

Part III. Other Activities Common to All the Classes

1. Organising exhibitions in coordination with nearby high/higher secondary schools and other institutions on topics such as:
   (a) Lives of saints and seers
   (b) Lives of scientists and their discoveries/achievements
   (c) Health and nutrition
   (d) Culture
   (e) Architecture, and
   (f) Science games.
2. School day celebration giving opportunities to pupils to express their talents and to bring their parents and community to the school.
3. Annual sports day.
4. Field trips to temples, farms and other places.
5. Organising filmstrip shows on topics related to the development of ethical and social values.
6. Dramatisation.
7. Drawing competitions.
8. Collection of pictures, stamps, hobbies, albums, etc.
9. Listening to select radio programmes.
10. Inviting or seeing great personalities who have a healthy message for the nation.

Guide-Book

In order to inculcate ethical and social values through education, a guide-book for the teachers is essential. This guide-book should have the following characteristics. It should be:

1. In the regional language.
2. Based on the experiences of primary school teachers and evolved through their participation. The responsibility of preparing the guidebook should be shouldered by a committee consisting of primary school teachers, teacher training experts and experts in child development.
3. Planned to include:
   (a) details regarding how the activities mentioned in Part I should be organised, conducted and evaluated;

(b) instructional material in the form of stories, drama and saying which could be introduced in the different classes;
(c) relevant visual aids which can be used along with the stories or actions to accompany songs to make the programme interesting;
(d) how the inculcation of values can be correlated with the subjects taught in the school; and
(e) a proforma for observing the behaviour of children to evaluate how far the values inculcated have taken roots and are reflected in their behaviour.

Orientation to Teachers

All the teachers should be oriented to inculcation of values through the values integrated approach to education.

The best period for orientation is just before the reopening of the schools after the summer vacation.

The duration of the orientation course may be about a fortnight (about 15 days).

Such training should become a regular part of all future teachers' training programmes.

The orientation programme should aim at the following:

1. An assessment of the values cherished by the teachers before and after orientation.
2. Developing skills in:
    (a) preparing instructional material
    (b) conducting group activities
    (c) telling stories effectively
    (d) singing songs
    (e) correlating values with the curricular subjects
    (f) training in observing children's behaviour

III. Secondary and Higher Secondary Stage

Objectives

To help pupils to:

1. inculcate ethical and social values and achieve moral development.
2. react to the environment.
3. create an awareness of the social environment and how to adjust to it.

4. understand the importance of religion.
5. become useful citizens.

The syllabus is given in two parts:

Part I—The content and methodology, and

Part II—How to integrate the ethical and social values with the school subjects

Part I. Content and Methodology)

	Content	How to teach
1.	Family, society, culture and religion as deciding factors	Stories from the epics, *Ramayana* and *Mahabharata*, life of seers and saints belonging to all religions not emphasising orthodoxy but human qualities and achievement
2.	Habit formation—character and conduct, choice of friends, acquisition of virtues, power to think developing qualities of head and heart	Regularity, punctuality, submitting assignments in time, observing study hours, eating meals at regular times, study and pray at regular times, visit to hospitals, temples, slums, temple adoption programmes, conducting night classes, helping in the orderly conduct of big temple festivals
3.	Discrimination between:	
	(a) Right and wrong, good and bad, distinction between legality and morality	Tirukkural, Gandhiji's life (*My Experiments with Truth*)
	(b) Discussion of moral, immoral and non-moral acts and what makes an act moral or virtuous	Discussing special incidents in the school
4.	Reaction to environments, better use of eyes and ears, powers of observation, attention/reasoning	Red Cross, Bharat Scouts and Guides, NCC, intramural and inter-school sports, school assemblies national days
5.	Cultivation of will power, perseverance, self-control and self-analysis	Swami Vivekananda and Karmayoga
6.	Neighbourliness, fairplay, natural help, cooperation	Jesus Christ and Gandhi
7.	Institutions, ideals and traditions, life at the institution, purposeful learning	Discussing the history of the institution, its motto, emblem, the duty of the pupils and what is expected of them at school

	Content	How to teach
3.	Discrimination between: (a) Right and wrong, good and bad, distinction between legality and morality	Tirukkural, Gandhiji's life (*My Experiments with Truth*)
	(b) Discussion of moral, immoral and non-moral acts and what makes an act moral or virtuous	Discussing special incidents in the school
4.	Reaction to environments, better use of eyes and ears, powers of observation, attention/reasoning	Red Cross, Bharat Scouts and Guides, NCC, intramural and inter-school sports, school assemblies national days
5.	Cultivation of will power, perseverance, self-control and self-analysis	Swami Vivekananda and Karmayoga
6.	Neighbourliness, fairplay, natural help, cooperation	Jesus Christ and Gandhi
7.	Institutions, ideals and traditions, life at the institution, purposeful learning	Discussing the history of the institution, its motto, emblem, the duty of the pupils and what is expected of them at school
8.	Country: The glorious past, the present situation, patriotism, customs, corporate living, unity in diversity, growth of cultures and civilisation with reference to ethics	Discussing: Constitution of India, Indian history, great epics, enacting some episodes from these works
9.	Citizenship: Concept of citizenship, what it means to be a citizen of the world. Basic human values-norms, duties and rights-relevance and significance of relief work during famine, floods, wars, earthquakes and other disaster	History of other nations, study of literature—especially dramas and poetry. Quiz in geography and historical points, collection of old clothes and donating them to the affected. Donating to mid-day meal programmes and other social activities.
10.	What does the society expect of me? What do I expect the society to provide me with to enable me to become a good citizen?	Lives of Socrates and Abraham Lincoln
11.	Social environment. Necessity for rules, obedience to the law, the concept of liberty, treating humanity as end and never as a means.	Gandhiji's satyagraha movement and his eleven vows discussing the importance of law in society

(*Contd.*)

	Content	*How to teach*
12.	Religion as background—what is religion?	The basic tenets common to all religions Rituals, prayers and fastings, their place and significance – Ramzan, Ekadashi, Good Friday and others. Teaching of different religions, meaning of the concept of the brotherhood of man
13.	Study of the lives and teachings of great teachers of the world	Lives and teachings of: 1. Krishna 2. Buddha 3. Jesus 4. Guru Nanak 5. Mohammed 6. Chaitanya 7. Sri Rama Krishna 8. Tiruvalluvar 9. Alwars and Nayanmars of Tamil Nadu 10. Ramalinga Adigal 11. Gandhiji 12 Swami Vivekananda; and 13. The Holy Mother.

Part II. Integrating Ethical and Social Values Through School Subjects

Value	*Content*	*Activity*	*To be integrated with*
Punctuality	Incidents from the lives of Gandhi, Nelson, "Little Things" from Samuel Smiles	(a) Following the daily routine (b) Returning library books in time (c) Attending school after vacation in time (d) Remitting school and other fees in time; and (e) Submitting assignments in time	History and language. These values may be integrated through other subjects also
Orderliness	Films: Road sense Mr. X Chart: Showing Road signs	(a) School assembly (b) Flag hoisting (c) NCC activities (d) Mass drill (e) Kit inspection (f) Waiting for one's turn in the bus stand, railway station (g) Exhibitions (h) Road sense (i) Excursions	Physical Education, Science and Geography

Value	*Content*	*Activity*	*To be integrated with*
Patriotism	India—George Washington, Abraham Lincoln Mazzini, Garibaldi, Gandhi, Swami Vivekananda, Jawaharlal Nehru, Tilak, Gokhale, A.O. Chidambaram, Subramaniam Bharathi, Rabindranath Tagore, songs from Sangam Literature: Purananooru, Thirukural	(a) Celebration's of national days (b) Celebration of the birth days of great leaders (c) Flag hoisting (d) Visits to places of national importance (e) Learning and singing of patriotic songs	History, geography language; and science
Respect for elders	Stories from *Ramayana*, *Mahabharata*, *Puranas*, War and Peace, Incidents that shaped great men	(a) Greeting parents, elders, teachers on various occasions (b) Courteous speaking in discussions and conversations (c) Offering seats to elders in trains and buses (d) Helping elders in their work	Languages
Non-violence	Incidents from lives of Buddha, Mahavira, Gandhiji and Martin Luther King	(a) Keeping pets (b) Maintaining albums of pictures of great people (c) Collecting sayings of great people	Language: History, Drawing and Painting
Faith in God	Life history of saints who have experienced God: Sri Ramalinga Vallalar, Swami Vivekananda, Appar, Sambandar, Andal and others, The Universe	(a) Daily prayers *bhajans*, meditation (b) Celebration of religious festivals (c) Spiritual retreats (d) Pilgrimage (b) Swimming (c) NCC activities	Language

Value	*Content*	*Activity*	*To be integrated with*
Fearlessness	Episodes from *Ramayana*, *Mahabharata* and *Puranas*. Life histories of great heroes like Shivaji, Kattabomman, Tensingh, Kumaran, Keller, Mehar Sen, Swami Vivekananda. Space travels and persons connected with them	(a) Hiking (b) Swimming (c) NCC activities	History Language and Science
Dignity of labour	Lives of Tolstoy, Gandhi, Edison, Benjamin Franklin, Michael Faraday	(a) Community work (b) Social service (c) Work projects in school (d) Self-help (e) Celebration	History Languages Science Arts and Craft
Truthfulness	Story of Harichandra, life of Gandhi, stories from Upanishads	(a) Dramatisation (b) Reading (c) Discussion	History Languages
Devotion to duty	Incidents from wars, stories depicting the value of duty	(a) Assigning responsibilities to pupils (b) School cabinet (c) Student' council (d) Celebrations (e) NCC activities	History Languages

Guide-books

Suitable guide-books should be prepared by experts and teachers for indication of ethical and social values. Workshops may be organised for a fortnight in pioneering educational centres with the coparation of national organisations like NCERT, Home Science Colleges and Teacher's Training Institutes and Colleges.

Research should be sponsored for the collection and evaluation of material for the guide-books; facilities should be given to voluntary agencies for the purpose. The material should include details of bravery awards, lives of scientists, literary men, institution builders, saints and seers, highlighting their qualities and achievements.

Help schools undertaking projects for preparation of aids, such as social and ethical value posters and filmstrips.

Suitable orientation programmes be organised for a period of one or two weeks, for teachers in all the educational institutions, for the inculcation of moral and social values.

Note: Suitable adjustments keeping in view the cultural background of the state/region may be added. However, while doing so, it should be ensured that national perspective is not diluted.

MODULE II: SUGGESTIVE PROGRAMME FOR THE TEACHING OF HUMAN VALUES IN SCHOOLS: OBJECTIVES, CURRICULUM AND METHODS

Objectives of Teaching Human Values

The Moral Education Committee of Uttar Pradesh (1983) which has equated moral education with value education has suggested the following general objectives:

(a) to promote in children such basic and fundamental qualities as truthfulness, cooperation, love and compassion, peace and non-violence, courage, equality, justice, dignity of labour, common brotherhood of man, and scientific temper;
(b) to train children to become responsible citizens in their personal and social lives;
(c) to enable them to understand and appreciate the national goals of socialism, secularism and democracy and to contribute to their realisation;
(d) to create in them an awareness of the socio-economic conditions and to motivate them to improve the same;
(e) to enable them to become open and considerate in their thought and behaviour and rise above prejudices based on religion, language, caste or sex;
(f) to develop their creative faculty, refine their aesthetic responsibility and quicken their imagination, broaden their vision, and enlarge their sympathies;
(g) to help them understand and appreciate themselves and continually strive for their inner development and becoming, thus moving towards the goal of self-actualisation; and
(h) to develop in them proper attitudes:

(i) towards oneself and fellow beings;
(ii) towards one's own country;
(iii) towards people of other countries, leading to international understanding;
(iv) towards life and environment; and
(v) towards all religions.

Stagewise Specific Objectives

Classes I and II

To enable the children:

(i) to acquire proper habits, such as, personal cleanliness and hygiene, regularity and orderliness;
(ii) to acquire social qualities, such as ability to work and play with others in harmony, sharing things, etc.;
(iii) to behave in a polite and well-mannered way towards parents, teachers and others;
(iv) to learn to speak the truth; and
(v) to be kind to animals, birds, etc.

Classes III–IV/V

The qualities earlier mentioned for the previous stage will be reinforced.

To enable the children:

(i) to acquire the habit of punctuality;
(ii) to practise honesty in word and deed;
(iii) to develop considerate and helpful attitude towards others;
(iv) to develop the spirit of courage, cooperation and team work;
(v) to love to do manual work and develop necessary elementary skills for it; and
(vi) to create and appreciate what is beautiful in the school and in the environment.

Classes VI–VII/VIII

The qualities earlier mentioned for the previous two stages will continue to get reinforcement.

To enable children:

(i) to develop patriotic, social and democratic values;
(ii) to develop a sense of duty and responsibility, devotion and perseverance;
(iii) to develop tolerance and to be open to others' views and

opinions;
(iv) to understand and appreciate Indian culture and civilisation;
(v) to promote national integration and unity; and
(vi) to imbibe sense of conservation of resources and preservation of environment including the preservation of wildlife.

Classes VIII–IX/X

Values mentioned in the previous stages will continue to receive reinforcement.

To enable the children:

(i) to imbibe values of truthfulness, self-discipline, peace, contentment and cheerfulness;
(ii) to shun evils such as cheating, corrupt practices, destruction of national property, false pride, taking of drugs, etc.
(iii) to practise equality in real life situations;
(iv) to develop an openness of mind and shed away prejudices of caste, creed, language and sex;
(v) to develop a secular outlook, respecting all religions and profit from their common teachings;
(vi) to imbibe a deep sense of humanism and love for all mankind and to draw inspiration from lives of great persons;
(vii) to develop creativity and scientific temper; and
(viii) to appreciate and accept the necessity for population stabilisation in the context of national development.

Classes XI–XII

Values mentioned in the previous stages will continue to receive reinforcement.

To enable the students:

(i) to become useful, productive members of society and strive to improve their productivity, contributing to both personal fulfilment and national development;
(ii) to explore their full potential and develop it in a continuous process of becoming and moving towards the goal of self-actualisation; and
(iii) to become a life-long learner.

This is only suggestive and much discretion should be left to teachers and heads in terms of the capacity of their students and the local factors.

Guidelines for Preparing the Curricular

(a) Value education should start with the first year of schooling and continue throughout.

(b) The curriculum would have an *integrated approach.*
- — integrating value education with as many subjects in the curriculum as possible;
- — integrating it with the whole of school programme;
- — integrating it with the co-curricular activities including sports and games;
- — integrating the value education programme with school climate and environment as well as with the lives and values of those in the institution;
- — integrating the life and concerns of the students with the real life situations and concerns of society; and

(c) The emphasis on this curriculum is on developing desirable attitudes in children rather than imparting mere information about values.

(*Report of the Moral Education Committee*, Uttar Pradesh, 1983. Based on the NCERT Paper '*Guide for the Curriculum of Moral Education in Schools*')

ROLE OF THE TEACHER IN VALUE DEVELOPMENT

Traditionally teachers are regarded as the torch bearer of the race and the makers of history. Although their role in this respect has diminished still it must be admitted that they exercise their considerable influence on children.

Teachers to be functional as vehicles of values must themselves be value-oriented. It has been remarked by a great thinker that if a teacher is devoid of values, it is better to take to shopkeeping. Gandhiji has observed,

"The secret of teaching values is to inspire and kindle the quest among the students by means of one's own example of character and mastery of knowledge. It is by embodying values within themselves that the teachers can really radiate values to their students."

All occasions of daily life should be utilised by the teacher to bring his student nearer to the realisation of the ideals. There are occasions when children express wild impulses and passions, and often they are in revolt. Children have their own daily battles of loyalties and friendship, and there are moments of desperate depression and of violent enthusiasm. There are occasions when children get vexed, become sulky and go on strike. All these occasions are occasions for value-oriented education. With patience and perseverance, the teacher can utilise all these occasions to show the truth and light and to awaken among the children the right sense and the right direction of true progress.

It must be remembered that values cannot be taught in the same way as lessons of information related to formal school subjects. Instruction should form a minor role, and a major role should be assigned to intimate contact and individual guidance. The role of the teacher is to put the child on the right path and to encourage him in his growth by watching, suggestions and helping, but not imposing or interfering.

Guidelines for Developing Values Among Students

In his book '*Eternal Education*,' C.P. Khanna (1990) has suggested the following guidelines for developing values among students:

1. It may first be noted that a good many children are under the influence of their inner psychic and spiritual being which shows itself very distinctly at times in their spontaneous turning towards truth, beauty and goodness. To recognise this turning and to encourage it wisely and with a deep sympathy would be the first indispensable step.
2. The most important quality to develop among the children is sincerity.
3. This quality and several other qualities are taught infinitely better by example than by beautiful speeches.
4. The undesirable impulses and habits should not be treated harshly. The child should not be scolded. Particularly, care should be taken not to rebuke a child for a fault which one commits oneself. Children are very keen and clear-sighted observers: they soon find out the educators' weaknesses and note them without pity.
5. When a child commits a mistake, one must see that he confesses it to the teacher spontaneously and frankly; and

when he has confessed it, he should be made to understand with kindness and affection what was wrong in movement and that he should not repeat it. A fault confessed must be forgiven.

6. A child should be encouraged to think of wrong impulses not as sins or offences but as symptoms of curable disease which can be remedied by a steady and sustained effort of the will-falsehood being rejected and replaced by truth, fear by courage, selfishness by sacrifice, malice by love.
7. Great care should be taken to see that unformed virtues are not rejected as faults. The wildness and recklessness of many young natures are only overflowing of an excessive strength, greatness and nobility. They should be purified, not discouraged.
8. When a child asks a question, he should not be answered by saying that it is stupid or foolish, or that the answer will not be understood by him. Curiosity cannot be postponed, and an effort must be made to answer questions truthfully and in such a way as to make the answer comprehensible to the student's mental capacity.
9. The teacher should ensure that the student gradually begins to become aware of his deeper self and that with this growing awareness the student is able to harmonise and resolve his inner conflicts.
10. It should be emphasised that if one has a sincere and steady aspiration, a persistent and dynamic will, one is sure to meet in one way or another, externally by study and instruction, internally by concentration, revelation or experience, the help that one needs. Only one thing is absolutely indispensable, namely, the will to discover and realise. This discovery and this realisation should be the primary occupation of the being, the pearl of great price which one should acquire at any cost. Whatever one does, whatever one's occupation and activity, the will to find the truth of one's being and to unite with it should always burn like fire behind all that one does, thinks and feels.
11. At higher levels of development, teacher should use the methods of daily conversation and books read from day to day. Books should contain lofty examples of the past, given not as moral lessons but as things of supreme human

interest. These books should also contain (a) great thoughts of great souls, (b) passages of literature which set fire to the highest emotions and promote the highest aspirations, and (c) records the history and biography which exemplify the living of great thoughts, noble emotions and inspiring ideals.

12. Opportunities should be given or created which would enable students to embody progressively higher and nobler values.

DEVELOPMENT OF VALUES AND ROLE OF THE HOME

There is an old Sanskrit '*Shloka*':

Matra devo bhava, pitra devo bhava
Guru devo bhava
(Mother is God, father is God, and teacher is God)

Indian tradition gives the highest precedence to the mother, then to the father and then to the teacher. In India, the mother has always been given a position of pre-eminence.

Throughout history of mankind, the greatest influence in building of character of a person good or bad has been the mother. Destiny of individuals is made or marred by mothers because very often, they are the ones who determine the path that their children will take in life. It is they who leave an indelible impression on the minds of their children by their behaviour, by what they tell them whether it is in terms of stories, fables or incidents from their own lives. If the home has an environment of hatred and violence, it permeates into the child's psyche. If the mother is an instrument of joy, happiness and bliss in the home, the child will always smile and radiate happiness.

DIFFICULTIES AND PROBLEMS IN PROMOTING VALUE EDUCATION

Among the various factors for not achieving the desired results in the promotion of value education or giving value orientation to education are:

— Lack of clarity of the concept, definition and meaning of value education.
— Lack of clarity on the conceptual framework.

— Non-availability of suitable learning/teaching materials and training modules,
— A tendency to treat value education as yet another subject,
— Lack of administrative inputs,
— Absence of any orientation programme for teacher educators, key-level personnel and schoolteachers,
— Overall environment of suspicion,
— Lack of role models in different walks of life.

CONSTRAINTS IN HUMAN VALUE EDUCATION

It is observed that the school is not the only place or the environment or the community in which a boy or girl lives, nor it is the only influence to which he is exposed. Out of twenty-four hours, he spends about six to seven hours in school. He spends more time outside the school than he does at the school. He is exposed to many influences which may reinforce the influence of value education in school or nullify it. There are many agencies which influence students. The first and most powerful influence is that of the home. It is here that *Sanskaras* are developed. Home environment determines the early and basic formation of character, attitudes to life, good and bad manners and the sense of value, however rudimentary. Now home education and training is neglected considerably and very little attention is paid to the moral and intellectual development of the child. Formerly there was, apart from the parents, the institution of grandmothers, who had time and inclination to feed the mind of the child with stories full of moral teaching. These also had the effect of integrating the child with his country and passing on to him some of its heritage. The institution of grandmothers seems to have broken down, and parents have little time for their children. This void is difficult to fill. This increases the need of teacher-parent relationship and it is recommended that methods and procedures should be devised to associate the parents with the school so as to interest them in the education of their wards. Apart from the annual parents' day, constant touch with parents be maintained by the school and parents kept informed how their wards are shaping and suggestions given as to what steps are required at the home. Some schools are doing this.

Then there is the influence of mass media on development of values.

Rapid advances in scientific and technological developments have been instant and mass communication an important fact of our everyday life. While no person is immune from the influence of mass media, the young of impressionable age are especially susceptible. Wisely regulated, this mass media can be made an instrument of developing the young minds in the right and desirable directions. But unfortunately, as matters stand at present, this mass media is more often than not, has corrupting influence on the youth, by and large. It sometimes glorifies violence and presents sex in a manner that has unhealthy effect on the minds of the young. The radio and the television, if properly used can be an important instrument to value education. It is very necessary that they should be regulated in society's interest. We are not against freedom of expression, nor suggest restriction on or control of the artists' right to create and present a picture or view of society, nor do we suggest that violence or sex can always be excluded from any story about human life. But we do recommend that considering the very powerful influence which the cinema and television exercise on the thoughts of a very large number of people, they should be prevented from corrupting the morals, the thoughts and sentiments of the people. Being audio-visual their influence is immediate and there is a special justification for regulating it, without killing the artists' creative expression. Commercialisation of female beauty and glorification of violence are not necessary to secure artists' or entertainers' right to create and to please. They corrupt the youth. Young minds are so conditioned by the cinema, television, radio and sometimes newspapers and magazines that value education given in school is very often ineffective in disabusing their minds of this ill-effect. Young men committing crimes have, during police interrogation, sometimes admitted that for planning the crime, they got the inspiration and ideas from these sources. It is recommended that a serious view of this be taken and corrective measures taken if the programme of value education is to be given a fair start.

Socio-economic conditions greatly influence moral behaviour. Poverty and morality cannot co-exist There is a Sanskrit saying: "What sin does a hungry man not commit?" People deprived of basic human needs such as food, clothing, health services and kindness and sympathy become frustrated and value education is wasted on them; it can have no effect. Indeed the whole set-up of a society, the values and ideals on which it is based matters. If the society is just, free from discrimination of caste and race, if there is a just distribution of wealth, then an environment exists which promotes value education. On the other hand, if the society is unjust, based on exploitation, then the best planned value education curricula will fail in achieving their objectives because of the contradictions inherent in the environment of which school is a part. A student cannot be effectively educated in values when he sees and experiences the opposite in the society at large. Values taught in the school can have no impact on the minds and actions of the students who see the negation of those values in the market place, at home, in Government offices and above all among the politicians who rule the country. Even though values be proclaimed at these places, but they are not practised and the young mind is quick to know this dichotomy between precept and practice. When he sees corruption and hypocrisy all round, school-taught value education is not going to have any appreciable impact on him. On this topic the Report of the Joint Study (1980) says: "The fundamental dilemma between precept and practice is reflected in the gap that exists between moral teaching and moral climate of school and society. This is clearly underlined by the corruption in some political and commercial groups. For morals to be so internalised that they influence judgment and action within and outside the school, the narrowing of this gap between precept and practice is essential. In fact, there is an occasional feeling that very strict inculcation of the principles of honesty and integrity in pupils may fail in some ways to equip them adequately for the realities of life outside the school. A serious attempt should therefore be made to resolve the dichotomy between precept and practice of morality."

Value education requires that there should be freedom of thought and expression. It aims at the moral development of the individual not only as part of society but also as a person in his own right. Full moral development of a child cannot take place if he is all the time weighted down by authority. Teaching of human values should be so devised that it encourages children to think for themselves, reason out the "why" and accept a preposition with full understanding and personal conviction. As we have pointed out earlier, true morality must not be presented as a dictate of somebody, whether it be parent, teacher or God. The development of the individual has to be in harmony with the needs of society; the needs of the two are, truly understood, not in conflict, but should there appear a conflict, this has to be solved by choosing the greater good of the greater number.

Some restraints will have to be imposed to begin with until they become habits. Such a restraint is in respect of one of intoxicants ranging from alcohol to hard drugs. This be done by creating an awareness in the students of the ill effect of intoxicants and drugs and the dangers of such addiction. The use of these intoxicants seriously interferes with the moral education programme and we are of the view that governmental action is also called for here.

Concluding Observations

The issue may be summed up with the observation of the Report of the Moral Education Committee UP (1983).

"We write about these constraints not because we take a pessimistic view about the value of moral education but because we want to state realities— realities which have a great impact on our subject. Making any class of members of a society moral must touch on the morality of others; there cannot be quarantine arrangements. The prevailing tone of entire society has to be moral. Seen from this point of view, we have an overall gloomy picture of Indian society today. But a beginning has to be made somewhere. The more difficult and complicated the problem, the greater the challenge, greater and more determined should be our response. It is better to light a candle than to curse darkness. It is only appropriate that the beginning is made from the school, for it is at the school that we catch them young. Herein lies the importance of introducing value education in our schools."

EVALUATION OF HUMAN VALUES

Evaluation is an integral element of human value education programme. Any programme of instruction and training to be effective, it is imperative to appraise the products of educational efforts. Since value education development programmes in general aim at developing not only formative but operational values as well, it is necessary to examine the evaluation techniques and procedures used in assessing progress towards the objectives of the instructional and training programmes. There is no doubt that evaluation procedures and instruments are as important as teaching. They should reflect the image of the human evaluation education programmes.

The very nature of the human value education requires that evaluation procedures are different from the education for knowing. Human value education is an education for 'becoming.' It is, therefore, necessary that formal procedures should not be considered adequate for this purpose. Here the observations of the teachers play the most important part.

The evaluation programme has to be a continuous one. The following evaluation measures can be adopted:

1. Paper-pencil tests
2. Teacher observation
3. Peer evaluation
4. Parent evaluation
5. Self-evaluation
6. Aptitude scales
7. Check lists
8. Situational performance tests
9. Activity-based questions
10. behaviour tally charts
11. Oral tests.

Formal and Information Evaluation

Broadly speaking, evaluative tests may be classified as formal procedures and informal procedures. Formal procedures will include objective and essay tests and two performance tests.

Objective and Essay Tests

These are to test student's knowledge and understanding of the moral values to be cultivated and traits of character to be developed. It is necessary to test this knowledge. Even though such knowledge by itself does not make character, it is a necessary first step to that desirable end. If the student has taken pains in properly learning and understanding values, the lesson must sink in his mind and set him thinking. This is a necessary exercise preliminary to further progress. These objective tests can be of several kinds. We give some examples below:

I. Multiple Choice Items and Essay Tests:

Example: What do you do when your friend has failed in the examination?

(i) Console him
(ii) Leave him alone
(iii) Ridicule him

Answer to this will reveal the kind of moral behaviour developed by the student answering the question.

Another type of question will reveal the reaction of the student to problems and critical situations.

Example: You are a policeman. You see your son committing theft. No one else is seeing. What would you do?

As regards essay tests, a subject be given to test the understanding of a particular value by the student.

Example: Write an essay on the importance of punctuality.

II. Performance Tests

In evaluating the impact of moral education, performance tests are more important than objective tests.

Example: Arrange a group activity and then watch what traits student participating exhibits. Two examples may be given:

Examples:

1. Take out the class for a picnic. Observe if—
   (i) students arrive in time and get into the bus in an orderly manner, forming a queue;
   (ii) get down in an orderly manner;
   (iii) wait for their turn in taking their share of snacks;
   (iv) leave or do not leave litter behind or pluck flowers or fruits in the park;
   (v) play the games in a sporting spirit; and
   (vi) play their part in collecting articles, boarding the bus in an orderly fashion.
2. Arrange a game or recreation and watch what qualities and traits of character the participating students exhibit.

While these formal procedures have their value in moral evaluation, their value is limited. On this point it may be noted that knowledge and awareness of the values, however, does not guarantee the practice of right conduct itself. Children usually respond to test situations which they think meet the teachers' approval and not necessarily as they would really have reacted and responded in a natural situation. In other words, children's responses to various types of tests—objective, essay and performance do not necessarily reflect the internalisation of the values developed.

It is, therefore, necessary to supplement the formal procedures with informal procedures.

Check list on human values may be kept maintained by the teacher.

Anecdotal records are straightforward and systematic descriptions of the actual behaviour of the students.

Inventories and questionnaires may be used. Students may be asked from time to time to indicate with examples the work done by them in acquiring values.

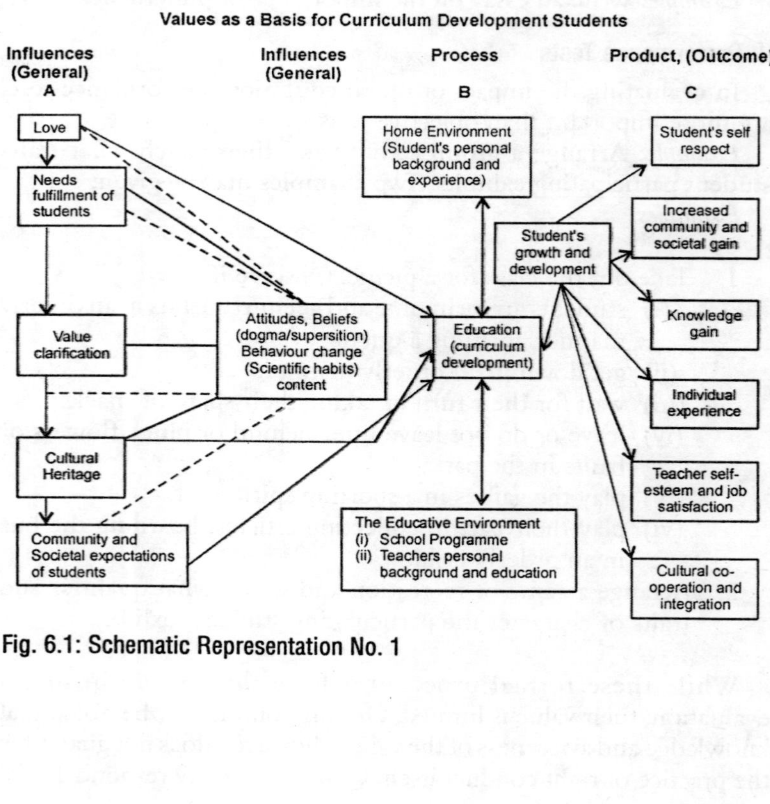

Fig. 6.1: Schematic Representation No. 1

Teacher's Role in Evaluation Process

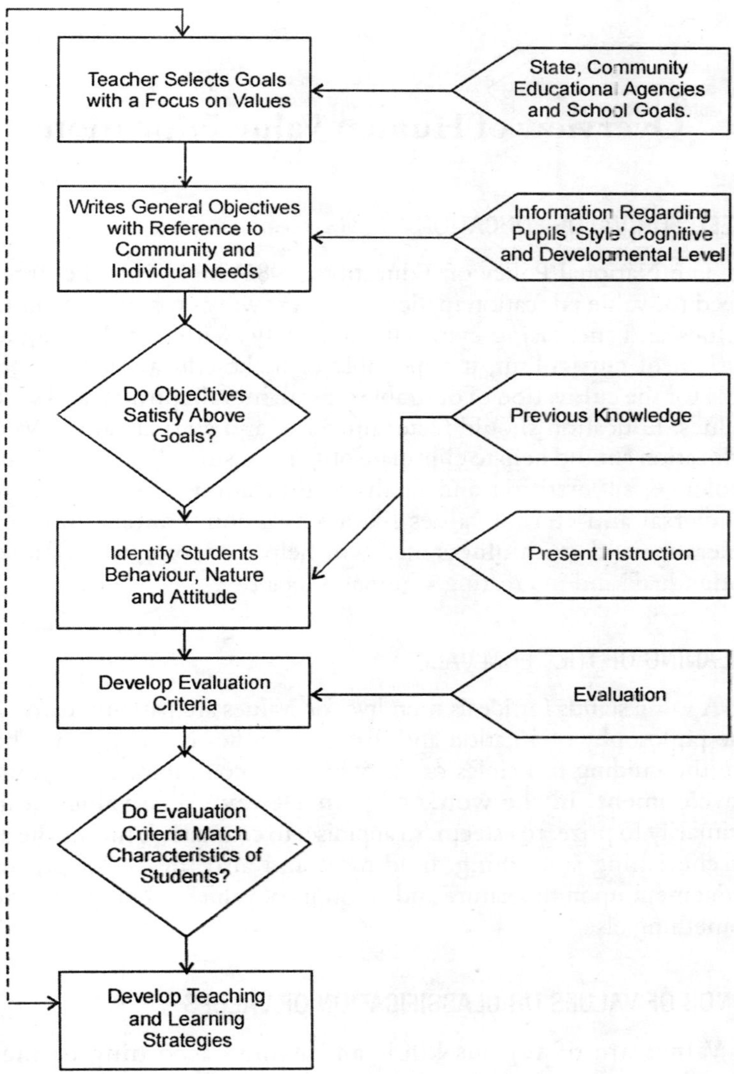

Fig. 6.2: **Schematic Representation No. II**

Source: Rajinder M. Kalra, *Value-Oriented Education in Schools: Theory and Practice*, Shipra, 2003.

7

Overview of Human Value Education

NEED FOR VALUE EDUCATION

The National Policy on Education (1986) highlights the urgent need for value education in view of the growing erosion of essential values and increasing cynicism in society. With a well-designed system of curriculum, it is possible to make education a forceful tool for the cultivation of desirable ethical, moral, spiritual and social values. Education should foster universal and eternal values. Value education should help to eliminate obscurantism, religious fanatism, violence, superstition and fatalism. Education which inculcates universal and eternal values like compassion, courage, honesty, tolerance and truthfulness etc., will help in developing balanced individuals and in creating a humane society.

MEANING OF THE TERM VALUES

A value stands for ideals men live for. Values are part and parcel of the philosophy of a nation and that of its educational system. They are the guiding principles of life which are conducive to all round development. In the words of John Dewey: "The value means primarily to prize, to esteem, to appraise, to estimate, it means the act of cherishing something, holding it and also the act of passing judgement upon the nature and amounts of values as compared with something else."

KINDS OF VALUES OR CLASSIFICATION OF VALUES

Values are of various kinds and named according to their specifications:

1. Aesthetic values in accordance with arts, dancing, painting, dramatisation, music etc.

2. Spiritual values concerning spirit as opposed to matter.
3. Moral values relating to ethics.
4. Social values concerning society.

EDUCATION AND NEED FOR INCULCATION OF VALUES

The Kothari Commission has rightly observed, "The expanding knowledge and the growing power (science) which it places at the disposal of modern society must, therefore, be combined with the strengthening and deepening of the sense of social responsibility and a keener appreciation of moral and spiritual values." Inculcation of desirable values in the pupils is felt essential for meeting out the crisis of character. In the situation that is rapidly developing, it is equally important for us to give a proper value orientation to our educational system.

FOUR MOST IMPORTANT HUMAN VALUES TO BE DEVELOPED IN STUDENTS: 4 D'S

1. Determination
2. Devotion
3. Discrimination
4. Discipline.

ROLE OF THE ENVIRONMENT IN VALUE DEVELOPMENT

The standards and norms adopted by people at home and in the immediate environment influence the child in shaping his moral behaviour. It is very unfortunate that often elders observe double standards of values. These double standards are observed by children. It is, therefore, every essential that elders set high standards of values.

Role of the Parents. What parents do in their daily life has a lasting effect on the minds of children. Home is the first place to influence the behaviour of the child.

Role of the Teacher. It has been stressed again and again that nothing can be more helpful in moulding the child's behaviour than the teacher's own conduct. A teacher has to set a high standard of behaviour before the child.

VALUE EDUCATION: CONTENTS AND METHODS OF IMPARTING VALUE EDUCATION

Some of the important ways of imparting value education are:

1. Examples should be taken from day-to-day life situations.
2. Extracts from sayings of great men should be explained.
3. Incidents and problems which develop value judgement should be taken up.
4. Inspirational dialogues, dramas, poems and material from religious scriptures could form the major part of the content of value education.
5. Biographies of great personalities should form an important source of value education.
6. Personal, neighbourly and community values should be taught in the classroom and thoroughly discussed with the students.
7. Yoga and other activities that develop self-discipline among students should be included.
8. Group activities like cleaning the school camps, visiting slums, service campus, visits to hospitals, visits to places of worship of different faiths should form part of content in value education.
9. Discourses on the lives of national and spiritual leaders can bring out values like self-sacrifice, collective happiness, love for truth and ultimate values of life for which the great leaders lived.
10. Prayer, meditation and '*Shramadan*' should form an integral part of the content of value education. They can help the students cultivate inner poise and an attitudinal shift, and develop the quality of 'dignity of labour.'
11. Observing birthdays of great national and spiritual leaders can go a long way in the inculcation of values in students.
12. A variety of learning resources can be used for value education. These may range from biographies, scriptures, proverbs, hymns and sayings of great persons.
13. A spirit of cooperative work and mutual help should prevail in the entire functioning of the school. In this regard, a major responsibility lies on the head of the school.

8

Documents on Human Values Education

This chapter includes the major recommendations of the following Committees and Commissions on human values education:

1. The Religious Education Committee (1946) appointed by the Central Advisory Board of Education, Government of India.
2. The University Education Commission (1948–49).
3. The Secondary Education Commission (1952–53).
4. Committee on Religious and Moral Education (1959).
5. The Education Commission (1964–66).
6. National Policy on Education (1986 and as amended in 1992).
7. Chavan Committee (1999).

RECOMMENDATIONS OF THE RELIGIOUS COMMITTEE APPOINTED BY THE CENTRAL ADVISORY BOARD OF EDUCATION (1946)

(i) The fundamental importance of the spiritual and moral values of life must be recognised in any scheme of education.

(ii) Spiritual and moral teaching common to all religions should be an integral part of the curriculum and provision of facilities for instruction therein should be a responsibility of the state.

(iii) An 'agreed' syllabus incorporating the spiritual and moral teachings common to all religions should be formulated.

(iv) In every school there will be every day a short period for meditation before the work of the day begins. The school should be assembled together for this period.

(v) Teaching in accordance with the fundamental levels of

different religions should primarily be the charge of the home or the community; but provision for this may be made in state schools by the community concerned, if there is a sufficient demand on the part of parents and guardians. Expenditure incurred on this account shall not be met from public funds.

(vi) If the alternative mentioned in (v) is availed of, the teachers employed for the purpose will conform to the minimum requirements regarding the qualifications and conditions of service for the other teachers employed in the institution.

(vii) The Central Advisory Board of Education be requested to set up a committee to investigate the best means of implementing the foregoing recommendations in respect of religious instruction at the various stages of education in state-provided, state-aided and recognised but not aided institutions.

Source: Goel, B.R., *Documents on Social, Moral and Spiritual Values in Education*, NCERT, 1979

RECOMMENDATIONS OF THE UNIVERSITY EDUCATION COMMISSION (1948–49)

The Commission headed by Dr. S. Radhakrishnan made the following observations and recommendations on value education and religious education.

Need for Religious Instruction

There are many who feel that morality can take the place of religion. We have to understand that the great virtues of loyalty, courage, discipline and self-sacrifice may be used for good or bad ends. These are essential for a successful citizen as well as for a successful villain. What makes a man truly virtuous is the purpose for which he lives, his general outlook on life. Virtue and vice are determined by the direction in which we organise our life. Unless morality is taken in a larger sense, it is not enough. If we exclude spiritual training in our institutions, we would be untrue to our whole historical development. India has believed that when one has done his duties as a *grahastha*, a householder has been a good father or mother, a good provider for the family, a good citizen, there is still the beauty and mystery of the universe, the meaning of life and death, the aspirations of the inner soul, that sad feeling of the wistful minded that beyond the world of positive knowledge there is a realm of forces unseen which we can feel but never know completely. (Para 6, page 299)

The fundamental principles of our Constitution call for spiritual training. There is no State religion. The State must not be partial to any one religion. All the different forms are given equal place, provided they do not lead to corrupt practices. Each one is at liberty to approach the Unseen as it suits his capacity and inclination. If this is the basis of our Secular State, to be secular is not to be religiously illiterate. It is to be deeply spiritual and not narrowly religious. (Para 29, page 300)

Practical Measures

If the education of the intellect divorced from the perfection of the moral and emotional nature is defective, how can it be improved? Religion cannot be imparted in the form of lessons. It is not to be treated as one of a number of subjects to be taught in measured hourly doses. Moral and religious instruction does not mean moral improvement. Instruction is not education. What can be tested in an examination is acquaintance with theories. What we need is not the imparting of instruction but the transmitting of vitality. We must civilise the human heart. Education of the emotions and discipline of the will are essential parts of a sound system of education. Religion is a permeative influence, a quality of life, an elevation of purpose. Our institutions, if they are to impart religious vitality, should have simplicity and an atmosphere of consecration that permanently influence lives. (Para 30, page 300)

Silent Meditation

A short period of silent worship or meditation, every morning before the class work starts, may well become an integral part of college life. For a few moments we may free the mind from the distractions of daily living and attend to the forces which determine the meaning and value of life. We will find the Supreme, the only Supreme, which it is possible for us to know, when we are taught to look within. "The spirit of man is the candle of the Lord." "Know you not that you are the temple of God and the spirit of God dwelleth in you" (St. Paul). These are variants of the famous text '*Tat twam asi*, 'that art thou.' The individual is a soul and the purpose of education is to awaken the pupil to this fact, enable him to find the spirit within and mould his life and action in the light and power of the inner spirit.

If religion means anything, it is that man is essentially a spiritual being. No one can be made moral or spiritual, unless these qualities are native to and inherent in man. (Para 31, page 300–301)

Study of Great Books

The attempt to make students moral and religious by the teaching of moral and religious textbooks is puerile. To instruct the intellect is not to improve the heart. Thought has an effect on life but there is the danger that we may make the thinking of morals and religions mechanical.

We must habituate the students to right emotions, induce in them the formation of good moral, mental and physical habits. Only what one accepts willingly becomes a part of oneself. All else is a mask.

How can we build the values into human mind? Our attempt should be to suggest and persuade, not command or impose. The best method of suggestion is by personal example, daily life and work and books read from day to day.

In the early stages, these books should contain not moral lessons but lives of great men given as things of supreme human interest, lives which exemplify the living of great thoughts and noble emotions. These books must be written with dignity, beauty and tenderness.

Education cannot ignore the great realities of experience and leave to chance their discovery by every young person. In the historic expressions of the fresh insights of great artists, we lift the hem of the garment of ineffable beauty. In the direct disclosures of the unutterable to the saint, we find persuasion and sustenance. In the moral claims and ethical formulations of the great social reformers, their upreaching spirit touches ours. Great literature sets fire to the highest emotions and prompts the highest ideals and aspirations. A study of great books, books that shame our smallness, that quell our fears, that fill us with hope, is essential in the university course. The Harvard proposals do not refer to religion on prudential rather than on educational grounds but they suggest a compulsory course in Humanities to be taken by every student during the first two years at college. They call it a study of the "Great Texts of Literature." Its aim is "familiarity with as much of the greatest writings as can be read and pondered in the limited time available. A list from which a selection would be made might include Homer, one or two of the Greek tragedies, Plato, the Bible, Virgil, Dante, Shakespeare, Milton, Tolstoy."

While in the secondary schools, stories which illustrate great moral and religious principles are used, in college classes, ideas, events and leading figures associated with religious movements should be studied. (Para 32, page 301)

Summary of the Recommendations

1. All educational institutions start work with a few minutes for silent mediation.
2. In the first year of the Degree course, lives of the great religious leaders like Gautama the Buddha, Confucius, Zoroaster, Socrates, Jesus, Sankara, Ramanuja, Madhava, Mohammad, Kabir, Nanak, Gandhi, be taught.
3. In the second year some selections of a universalist character from the Scriptures of the world be studied.
4. In the third year, the central problems of the philosophy of religion be considered. (Para 36, page 303)

RECOMMENDATIONS OF THE SECONDARY EDUCATION COMMISSION (1952–53) ON HUMAN VALUES EDUCATION

The Secondary Education headed by Dr. A. Lakshmanaswami which examined all aspects of secondary education made the following recommendations:

The Commission considered that healthy trends in regard to religious and moral behaviour spring from three sources:

1. The influence of the home which is the dominant factor;
2. The influence of the school through the conduct and behaviour of the teachers themselves and life in the school community as a whole;
3. Influence exercised by the public of the locality and the extent to which public opinion prevails in all matters pertaining to religious or moral codes of conduct.

No amount of instruction can supersede or supplant these three essential factors. Such instruction can be supplemented to a limited extent by properly organised instruction given in the schools. One of the methods adopted in some schools is to hold an assembly at the commencement of the day's session with all teachers and pupils present, when a general nondenominational prayer is offered. Moral instruction in the sense of inspiring talks given by suitable persons selected by the headmaster and dwelling on the lives of great personages of all times and of all climes will help to drive home the lessons of morality. (Page 126)

In view of the provisions of the Constitution of the Secular State, religious instruction cannot be given in schools except on a voluntary basis and outside the regular school hours; such instruction should be given to the children of the particular faith and with the consent of the parents and the managements concerned. In making this recommendation we wish to emphasise that all unhealthy trends of disunity, rancour, religious hatred and bigotry should be discouraged in schools. (Page 127)

RECOMMENDATIONS OF THE COMMITTEE ON RELIGIOUS AND MORAL EDUCATION (1959)

Introduction

The Ministry of Education, Government of India, appointed in 1959, a Committee on Religious and Moral Education, with Sri Prakasha as its Chairman. The terms of reference of the Committee were as follows:

(i) To examine the desirability and feasibility of making specific provision for the teaching of moral and spiritual values in educational institutions.

(ii) If it is found desirable and feasible to make such a provision, then, (a) to define broadly the content of instruction at various stages of education, and (b) to consider its place in the normal curriculum.

Observations of the Committee

Moral and Spiritual Values Defined

The Committee defined moral and spiritual values as follows:

'Anything that helps us to behave properly towards others is of *moral value*.' (Para 30)

'Anything that takes us out of our self, and inspires us to sacrifice for the good of others or for a great cause is of spiritual value.' (Para 30)

Need for the Teaching of Moral and Spiritual Values

We have to lay special stress on the teaching of moral and spiritual values. Moral values particularly refer to the conduct of man towards man in the various situations in which human beings come together in the home, in social and economic fields, and in the life of the outside world generally. It is essential that from the earliest childhood, moral values should be inculcated in us. We have to influence the home first. We fear that our homes are not what they ought to be. Habits, both of mind and body, formed in the early years at home, persist, and influence our life afterwards. Good manners are a very important part of moral education. It is not unusual that when a people attain freedom suddenly after long years of bondage, they are inclined to become self-willed, arrogant and inconsiderate. In such situations good manners are easily set aside and young people tend to express the first flush of freedom in license and rowdyism. (Para 25)

The importance of good manners cannot be overstressed. With the passing away of the old, aristocratic society of the nineteenth century, much of the graciousness and charm of social behaviour and human relationships has largely disappeared. To outsiders we often give the impression of being impatient and ill-mannered. Both in private and public life, we observe that due to mutual suspicion and prejudice, and preconceived notions and false ideas, much avoidable friction is caused. Good manners will impose proper restraint on us and remove harshness in our words and rudeness in our behaviour. Good manners verily are like the oil that helps to keep the machine of human society running smoothly. We have been losing our manners rather rapidly and it is necessary that we should recover them. Good manners should be sedulously inculcated and teachers must give instruction in this to all students at all times, both by example and by precept. We must be constantly told that what hurts us, hurts others also; and we must behave towards others as we want others to behave towards us. (Para 25)

Then there is a great deal of talk of corruption and dishonesty in our official and business life. It is the students of today who are to be in charge of the various departments of life tomorrow; and if they learn what real integrity is in their early years, they are not likely to go very far wrong later on. Every effort must, therefore, be made to teach students true moral values from the earliest stage of their educational life. We are not unaware of the various steps that are being taken at different educational levels towards literacy drive, adult education, and education of the handicapped. If the content of education is also enriched with moral and spiritual values, the purpose of education will have been truly fulfilled. (Para 26)

Just as moral values affect the relations between man and man, so do spiritual values affect the individual in his relation with himself. The individual is not only a body; he is also a soul. He does not live by bread alone; he wants inner peace and happiness. If he loses all spiritual values, he loses the possibility of being at peace with himself. It is necessary to have some faith in things beyond the flesh, some identification with a purpose greater than oneself in order to achieve this mental equilibrium. (Para 27)

Framework of Instruction on Moral and Spiritual Values in Education

The following suggestions merely indicate a broad framework of instruction in moral and spiritual values at different stages of education:

I. Elementary Stage

(a) The school assembly should be held for a few minutes in the morning for group singing.

(b) Simple and interesting stories about the lives and teachings of prophets, saints and religious leaders should be included in the syllabus for language teaching.

(c) Wherever possible the interest of the child may also be aroused by the use of audio-visual material, especially good quality photographs, filmstrips and coloured reprints showing great works of the main living religions of the world; such material could be used in the teaching of geography.

(d) In the school programme, two periods a week should be set aside for moral instruction. In these classes the teacher should relate interesting stories drawn from the great religions of the world and explain broadly their ethical teachings. Rites and rituals of religion should be excluded from moral instruction.

(e) Though school programme, the attitude of 'service' and the realisation that "work is workship" be developed in the child.

(f) All schemes of physical education and all forms of play in the school should contribute to the inculcation of the spirit of true sportsmanship.

II. Secondary Stage

(a) The morning assembly should observe two minutes' silence followed by readings from the scriptures or great literature of the world or an appropriate address. Community singing should also be encouraged.
(b) The essential teachings of the great world religions should be studied as part of the curriculum pertaining to social studies and history. Simple texts and stories concerning different religions may be included in the teaching of languages and general reading.
(c) One hour a week should be assigned to moral instruction. The teacher should encourage the habit of discussion in the class. Apart from this regular class instruction, suitable speakers may be invited to address the students on moral and spiritual values. Joint celebrations may be organised on the occasion of important festivals of all religions. Knowledge and appreciation of religions other than one's own and respect for their founders should be compulsory and physical education, including sex hygiene, should be a normal part of school programme.
(d) Qualities of character and behaviour of students should form an essential part of the overall assessment of a student's performance at school.

III. University Stage

(a) Students should be encouraged to meet in groups for silent meditation in the morning. These meetings should be supervised by the senior staff on a volunteer basis.
(b) A general study of different religions should be an essential part of the general education course in degree classes.

Concluding Observations of the Committee

"Our nation of tomorrow is going to be what the young people at school, college and university today will make it. The edifice of our future entirely depends for its beauty, dignity, utility and training that our youth receive. The New India, that is in the making, needs the services of us all—old and young, high and humble alike. If we neglect giving our boys and girls, our young men and young women, proper education and training, the future is dark and dismal indeed. We would regard our labours amply awarded, if by this report, we can help, in however small a measure, in the right orientation of our scheme of education so that our educational institutions—from the primary village school to the largest metropolitan university—may send forth year after year, and generation after generation, men and women fully trained and equipped to take their proper places in the different departments of national activity; and by their conduct, character and capacity, enhance the happiness and prosperity of our people, and keep the unity, integrity and freedom of the country, inviolate for all times to come."

RECOMMENDATIONS OF THE EDUCATION COMMISSION (1964–66)

Introduction

The Education Commission popularly known as the Kothari Commission after Prof. D.S. Kothari, the Chairman of the Commission, went into all aspects of education and suggested reforms for its reconstruction. Its observations on human value education are given below. It may be noted that the Commission did not use the term 'human value education.' However, the recommendations touch all aspects of human value education in varying degrees.

Observations and Recommendations

Social, Moral and Spiritual Values in School Curriculum

A serious defect in the school curriculum is the absence of provision for education in moral, social and spiritual values. In the life of majority of the Indians, religion is a great motivating force and is intimately bound up with the formation of character and inculcation of ethical values. A national system of education that is related to life, needs and aspirations of the people cannot afford to ignore this purposeful face of education. We recommend, therefore, that conscious and organised attempts be made for imparting education in social, moral and spiritual values with the help, wherever possible, of the ethical teachings of great religions. (Para 8.94, p. 358)

Moral Education through Indirect Methods

This education, we believe, should be provided, both by direct and indirect methods, by suggestion as well as by discussion and teaching.

We attach great importance to the role of indirect influence in building up good character. The school atmosphere, the personality and behaviour of the teachers, the facilities provided in the school, will have a large say in developing a sense of values. We would like to emphasise that the consciousness of values must permeate the whole curriculum and the programme of activities in the school. It is not only the teachers incharge of moral instruction who are responsible for building character. Every teacher, whatever be the subject he teaches, must necessarily accept this responsibility. He must ensure that in the teaching of his particular subject and in his dealings with his pupils, fundamental values such as integrity and social responsibility are brought out. The teacher need not, we can even say that he should not, try to draw out the underlying moral all the time; but if he has given some thought to the values underlying the scope of his subject and his work as a teacher, they will imperceptibly pass into his teaching and make an impact on the minds of his students. Moreover, a sense of purpose should inspire all school activities and must be reflected in the life, tone and atmosphere of the school. The school assembly, the curricular and co-curricular activities, the celebration of religious festivals of all religions, work-experience, team games and sports, subject clubs, social service programmes—all these can help in inculcating the values of cooperation and mutual regard, honesty and integrity, discipline and social responsibility. These values have a special significances in Indian society today, when young men and women are passing through a crisis of character. (Para 8.95, pp. 358–59)

Direct Instruction of Moral Values

In addition to this indirect approach for inculcating moral and spiritual values, we consider that specific provision for direct moral instruction in the school programmes is highly desirable. We agree with the recommendation of the Sri Prakasa Committee that one or two periods a week should be set aside in the school time-table for instruction in moral and spiritual values. At the primary stage such instruction will generally be imparted through interesting stories, including stories drawn from the great religions of the world. At the secondary stage, there may be frequent discussions between the teacher and the pupils on the values sought to be inculcated. Whatever be the method of teaching, it should not lead to moral instruction being divorced from the rest of the curriculum or being confined to a single period. If the values are to become a part of the student's character, an all-embracing treatment of the moral way of life is needed. (Para 8.96, p. 359)

Relation between Moral Values and Religion

There will be natural points of correlation between the moral values sought to be inculcated and the teachings of the great religions. Stories drawn from the great religions of the world will be most appropriate in a discussion of moral values and of problems in life. All religions stress certain fundamental qualities of character, such as honesty and truthfulness, consideration for others, reverence for old age, kindness to animals, and compassion for the needy and the suffering. In the literature of every religion, the story of parable figures prominently as a means of impressing an ethical value on the followers. The narration of such stories by the teachers at the right moment in the programme of moral education would be most effective, particularly in the lower classes. (Para 8.97, p. 359)

At a later stage, accounts of the lives of great religious and spiritual leaders will find a natural place. Some of these may be included in the study of social studies or literature, but it is essential that all important religions are represented properly in the programme. Similarly, the celebration of the festivals of different religions will afford opportunities for the narration of incidents from the life history of the leaders of these religions. In the last two years of the secondary school, a place should be found for the study of the essential teachings of the great religions. (Para 8.98, page 359)

NATIONAl. POLICY ON EDUCATION (1986 AND AS AMENDED IN 1992) ON HUMAN VALUES EDUCATION

(Already discussed)

RECOMMENDATIONS OF THE EIGHTY-FIRST REPORT ON VALUE-BASED EDUCATION (1999) DEPARTMENT RELATED PARLIAMENTARY STANDING COMMITTEE ON HUMAN RESOURCE DEVELOPMENT, POPULARLY KNOWN AS CHAVAN (S.B.) COMMITTEE

Observations and Recommendations

"Truth (*Satya*), Righteous Conduct (*Dharma*), Peace (*Shanti*), Love (*Prema*), and Non-Violence (*Ahimsa*) are the core universal values which can be identified as the foundation stone on which the value based education programme can be built up. These *five* are indeed universal values and respectively represent the five domains of human personality: intellectual, physical, emotional, psychological and spiritual. They are also correspondingly correlated with the five major objectives of education, namely, knowledge, skill, balance, vision and identity." (p. 2)

"It is very essential that at the school level right from the primary stage, deliberate, planned and sustained efforts are made to inculcate basic human values among the students. ...At this impressionable stage, values like respect for parents, elders and teachers, truth, punctuality, cleanliness and courtesy can be easily inculcated in small children. They can be sensitised regarding gender equality.

Besides the personal values there are certain social values which ought to be imbibed by the young mind. These are the values which concern the whole community: concern for the aged and the handicapped, for the deprived sections of the society, etc. Sincere belief in the dignity of labour is generally found to be lacking in our young generation. Values of self-dependence and insistence on doing manual work are thus required to be impressed upon small children." (pp. 2–3)

"It is essential that certain national values are also imbibed by the young students. They should be acquainted with the history of India's freedom struggle, cultural heritage, constitutional obligations and the features comprising our national identity." (p. 3)

"The process of making the students acquainted with the basics of all religions, the values inherent therein and also a comparative study of the philosophy of all religions should begin at the middle stage in schools and continue up to the university level. Students have to be made aware that the basic concept behind every religion is common, only the practices differ. Even if there are differences of opinion in certain areas, people have to learn to co-exist and carry no hatred against any religion." (p. 3)

"All the values are derived from ultimate reality—supreme power or self-consciousness—to which man orients himself. ...To believe that we have the divine spark in each one of us is the most important eternal value to be inculcated by the small children even before starting their school life." (p. 3)

"There has to be developed in students a feeling of respect for all languages of the country, if the concept of unity in diversity is to be effectively imbibed." (p. 3)

"The teacher is the key person who can inculcate all the required values in small children in spite of many odds. This task would become easier if the teacher through his personal character and actions sets an example before his students." (p. 3)

"Value education should be a part of curriculum for teacher training programme. Prospective teachers should be introduced to the concept of value education. All methods and techniques—both direct and indirect for inculcating values in students in tune with the different stages of their psychological development should be an essential component of teacher training programme. ...They need to be reoriented so that they may impart higher values to their pupils through example and through percept." (p. 4)

"School environment is to be consciously organised to expose students to values formally as well as informally... Morning assembly is a very effective medium of imparting values in students ... Meditation can also play a key role. Students can sit silently and reflect about their conduct and behaviour. They can learn to develop concentration and they can be made aware of the quiet strength lying within one's own body and mind."